The Call of God

Steve & Sally Wilson

The Call of God

AN INVITATION TO PARTNER WITH HEAVEN

Steve & Sally Wilson

globalawakening
lighting fires • building bridges • casting vision

The Call of God; An Invitation to Partner with Heaven by Steve and Sally Wilson

Apostolic Network of Global Awakening
1451 Clark Street
Mechanicsburg, PA 17055

For more information on how to order this book or any of the other materials that Global Awakening offers, please contact the Global Awakening Store.

ISBN: 978-1-944238-13-1

Contents

Endorsements

Working with Steve and Sally for the last 10 years has been an amazing expression of the Father's heart for developing anyone who is willing to walk in the fullness of their ministry calling. One of the primary distinctions of Steve and Sally's ministry is their belief and power in ministry pluralism. As I have walked with Steve and Sally they have been a massive encouragement to me and for me to walk fully in my five-fold calling.

It should come as no surprise that they not only believe in creating a platform within the church for every person to express their gift, but that they also promote and encourage that each individual can also operate in their God-designed platform and calling on a daily basis, outside of the church. Understanding that your calling may not have a "ministry" title meaning within the 4 walls of the church has been an incredible freedom for me and has enabled me to see the Holy Spirit work in unexpected ways in unexpected places through mediums that we would not normally consider an avenue of ministry. The truth is that even in the mundane moments of our everyday life we are operating in our ministries whether we know it or not. To believe it, gives the ministry power and adds excitement to every piece of our life.

This book helps dismantle the mindset that we minister at church and we work during the week. We are all called to ministry, but the ministry is every moment, in every place, at every time with every person we contact. Our job, our time, our money, our network. If you have never seen that before in your own life, this book will uplift and encourage you to see new possibilities and expressions of the Father's heart in every avenue of your life.

Ray VanDerLinden
Owner-operator of School of Racing Graphics

When we met over twenty years ago, I was running a graphic design studio and a sign shop. The church my wife and I had been attending had recently closed its doors, leaving us searching for direction. Steve and Sally gently helped us back on our feet, and soon we were leading the worship and the youth ministry at Dayspring. About that time, we had four children in diapers and one on the way (yeah, that is not a typo). I knew we had stumbled upon something unique when they sat us down and said, "We want to pay you for one day a week, and for that day we pay you, we want you to take it off and rest." They knew that the primary call of God on our lives – to enjoy communion with the Lord – was in jeopardy of drowning in a sea of activity.

I count it one of my greatest privileges to have known and worked side by side with Steve and Sally for the past two decades. They have spent their lives helping people like me answer God's invitation, the call to partner with Him in the work of the kingdom. As fathers in the current revival, they carry an unshakable passion to expand the kingdom of God with a heartfelt compassion for people and a deep commitment to biblical accuracy. I believe they will one day be listed among the great revivalists of church history.

They write in this book, "We often use the word 'call' exclusively for people who go into some kind of ministry vocation. But we want to kill that religious idea; it's a sacred cow that needs to die." In this book Steve and Sally kill that cow. The life-changing insights they share here I believe will send shockwaves through the church, getting people off the sidelines and into the action. They write, "We're not just waiting for something else to happen; we're allowing Him to use us to make things happen." Revival is following them again, out of the church walls and into every corner of society.

Farley Lewis
Artist, editor, graphic designer and muralist
Lead Pastor of Dayspring Eldorado Springs, MO

By reading this book, you are stepping into a manifesto of sorts, a spring of life from two people who have been living a radically surrendered life to God for longer than most people have been alive. It is a culmination of their learnings and reapings through the heat and friction of many trials and crucibles, including rejection by man, resistance from the world, and fierce spiritual warfare against their advances for the Kingdom. A very rare purity of character and wisdom has been forged in these fires, and what I so deeply appreciate is that they have taken the time to invite us into the forge with them.

As you read this book, I expect God's call will be quickened within you. But His call requires your ear to be pierced with an awl: A life freely and irrevocably given to Him. In other words, you're either "awl in" or "awl out"! May the words of God spoken through Steve and Sally become flesh in you, so that when your flesh is broken open like Jesus', His life will pour out of you and heal the nations.

Kurt Theobald
CEO, Nucleus Commerce & Classy Llama
Author of *Finding Truth at the Bottom*

Revival follows Steve and Sally Wilson. Dayspring the church they planted more than 20 years ago has become a revival center for the region and a force of influence all over the world. Revival is now following their spiritual sons and daughters. Some of these are pastors and ministry leaders, but many are carrying the flames of revival into the marketplace as businessmen, educators, entrepreneurs, homemakers, artists and politicians.

To live a life of fire does not require a title, but rather a calling from God. We are all called, regardless of the title or work place that we find ourselves in. I have seen cooks in a kitchen demonstrate the call of an evangelist, I have seen managers in a restaurant embody the call of a pastor, your title does not encompass your calling, your calling encompasses your life. Living a life of fire flows from one person leaning into the heart of God and coming out with vision, passion and direction. Each chapter of this book is filled with stories of people who choose not to live by their title, but rather their calling. Steve and Sally break down the wall between secular and sacred and empower people of every walk of life to step into their divine assignment and fulfill they're calling. Destroying false beliefs about calling being for the spiritual elite, and bringing it back to its scriptural premise; that we are all called.

Those who live from their calling in life, find themselves more fulfilled. Calling gives each person their divine purpose and purpose fuels our lives to live on purpose. Jesus selected fishermen and tax collectors, the ignored and the disliked to change the world. The moment before they heard the voice of Jesus and began to follow they were living task to task. The moment they began to follow Jesus they were living from glory to glory, meaning they were moving and growing towards their life agenda.

There is always an excuse not to fulfill your calling: your station in life, your financial situations, lack of opportunities, etc. however scripture is filled with people who regardless of their limitations fulfilled their divine calling. So if your life is riddled with difficulty you are a prime candidate to change the world. In the midst of the biggest conflict, God will pick the seemingly irrelevant character to turn everything around. He chose a shepherd boy to defeat a giant, and lead Israel, God chose a stuttering man to speak to His people on His behalf, God chose a man named Gideon who was hiding from his enemies while threshing wheat in a wine press to be a valiant warrior. God used fisherman and tax collectors to lead the greatest move of God in History. The roses are always among the thorns. It is interesting David's mighty men were the ragamuffins, the castaways of society, yet God finds a way to use the least to do the greatest deeds. We can either survey our lives and say we cannot live from our calling due to circumstances, or we can look at the God who called us and co-labor with Him to bring great and radical change to our lives and lineage.

Ahab Alhindi
Ahab & Jessica Alhindi Ministries
Author of *Limitless Intimacy*

Acknowledgements

We are grateful for our friendship with Randy Clark.
Thank you for your tireless pursuit of the presence and power of
God. You have had a lasting impact on our lives and we are forever
grateful for your sacrifice.

We are grateful to Aunt Bess who introduced Sally to Jesus.
We thank Dale Perkins who set us up for our first date; it was a
prank that backfired! Thank you both for profoundly changing the
course of our lives!

Special thanks to Farley Lewis
for proof reading, editing and valuable suggestions.

Special thanks to Melissa VanDerLinden
for the cover design and for formatting the book for us.

The Call of God
Introduction

The call of God is an invitation into a life of encounters with the Holy Spirit. God welcomes His people to find and live with a daily awareness of His call on their lives. When we use the term "call," we generally think of a call to preach or call to ministry. We assume that those who are "called" are either going to pastor a church or go to the mission field. But in scripture the word "call" has little to do with a specific ministry function; rather, the call of God is actually an appeal that extends to every believer in every moment and in every season of life. Yes, as we walk in our calling the Spirit will lead us into specifics, but it all starts with our individual response to His invitation.

The word "call" used in the New Testament basically means invitation, but the meaning also includes the idea of *to summon* or *to challenge*. Heaven's invitation is a summons to pursue a higher purpose and meaning for our life. It is a summons to respond to the call of God, which will unlock His ultimate purpose and plan for every person's life. The decision we all face is to respond to the invitation of our Creator to pursue a higher purpose and meaning for our life by saying yes to His call.

The call is also a challenge to go for more. The call of God leaves little room for complacency if we hope to become all He destined for us. No matter how far we have come or how much we have learned there is always more. The call of God is a challenge to pursue with our whole life, always hungry for more.

There's no arena of our life exempt from the call of God. So the call of God encompasses more than we've understood. If the priesthood of the believer is true, then every believer needs to surrender to the call of God. Every one of us should operate with an awareness that we are called to do whatever He asks. God called Smith Wigglesworth as a plumber and yet his stewardship of the call within his profession resulted in an incredible release of God's presence and power throughout his life of plumbing. Reese Howells called as a coal miner, yet God released intercessions through him that changed the scope of World War II, simply because he said yes to the call of God. God is calling us, pressing us, and challenging us to recognize the urgency of the call.

We believe this is a season for the full restoration of the priesthood of the believer - the time for the body of Christ to come alive and fulfill their calling and destiny. Peter tells us that we ...*are being built up as a spiritual house, a holy priesthood, to offer up spiritual sacrifices acceptable to God through Jesus Christ* (1 Pet 2:5). The people of God form the spiritual house He is building and as priests of this spiritual house we all minister to the Lord and minister to those around us on His behalf.

This truth, prophesied in the Old Covenant and now fulfilled under the New Covenant, has the power to destroy every artificial distinction that religion has created. No longer are we limited by a clergy/laity divide, or concerned about whether our work is secular or sacred. We need to stop wondering whether we should be full-time or part-time; the truth is that all believers are called to full-time availability. The call of God invites us to surrender our life, putting our time, energy and resources at His disposal.

If our will is bent to please God, then just do whatever He sets before us. Minister to the one in front of us; just do it. Meet the need He sets before us and in that moment we find that we're walking in the center of the call of God on our life; what an incredible privilege. Many beg, want, look for, and wait to know what they are called to, instead of just saying "yes." All we need to say is yes and in that act we step into our prophetic destiny. From the moment we say yes, every arena of our life is impacted by the call.

There's an invitation resounding from heaven. God looks throughout the earth for people willing to respond to His call. He is waiting with open arms, longing to draw us into a deeper relationship with heaven's purpose. God is inviting each of us into a partnership with Him that will impact and change the world we live in. That's the essence of the call of God.

In the chapters of this book we set out to explore the depth and breadth of the invitation heaven has extended to us. Sally and I have lived each of these chapters and have found ourselves having to say yes in some very difficult circumstances many times over the years. But we would not trade one moment of the joy and fulfillment of obedience to the call of God on our lives.

We have chosen to begin each chapter with a testimony from some of our friends. Each one shares their experience of some aspect of learning to fulfill their calling as a way of life and specifically in their work environment. They come from diverse backgrounds and widely varying professions, but all of them have discovered the truth that they are called. This revelation of the call of God on their lives reflects in the impact each has had on their marketplace.

The Call of God:
An Invitation to Enlist

Missy, an emergency room doctor writes – When my husband, Jeff, and I were first married, we struggled to understand our calling. I am a physician, left brained, analytical; he is an artist, right brained, creative. Then one day, sitting in a conference, we heard God say that He had called us "to bring peace, healing and wholeness in Jesus name!" That's our calling! I do that through medicine; he does it through art.

I am learning that my calling is to bring people the best of Jesus and the best of medicine. It does not have to be either/or. I am not just a Christian at church and a physician at work…I am a child of God everywhere, all the time. That is totally freeing! Before I understood my identity as a child of God, I tried to keep my professional life and personal life separate. Now I understand that I host the presence of God wherever I go; I don't have to try to separate my life. I host the Holy Spirit at work as much as I host Him at church!

One of my life verses is Deut 30:15, where Moses instructs God's people to "choose life" when they enter the Promised Land. Life for me came when I realized there is no separation between secular and spiritual, between work and faith.

1

An Invitation to All

The call of God is for every believer in every moment of the day and at every stage of life. It is our responsibility to simply respond and say yes. There is no arena of our life that we can afford to hold exempt from deliberate obedience to the call of God. When we surrender to the call, we enlist as carriers of the life of His Kingdom. The call of God provides a solid foundation for both our identity and for every thought and action. Hearing and obeying the call should become the primary motivation for every facet of our life. The call provides the reason we get up in the morning and gives meaning to our work. The call influences the way we treat people, because it opens our eyes to heaven's value system. There is something special about living with a sense of being called by God and knowing we have enlisted in His special forces. Recruited to partner with Him in fulfilling His purpose here on earth.

I can take you to the place where I was sitting in the bush in Kenya when I first heard the call of God. I had gone with my dad to help on a water project for another mission station. Late in the afternoon after we had finished work I climbed the hill behind us and sat down on a rock overlooking the valley below. What happened next was my first encounter with hearing the voice of God. To put this in perspective, my parents named me Steven Samuel, and in some of my earliest memories I recall them telling me they chose my names because they wanted me to hear God like Samuel and be willing to die for the Gospel like Stephen. It summed up my destiny.

As a child I lived with the idea that I should hear God speak but at the same time was taught by my parents from a cessationist point of view that God didn't talk to us anymore except through His Word. I marveled at the call of Samuel and remember wishing I could hear the Lord call my name. It often left me feeling disappointed and even robbed that something that life-transforming was now out of reach.

As I sat on the rock enjoying the incredible scenery, a hawk drifted by gliding on the breeze. It came close enough that I could almost reach out and touch it. I marveled at its ability to fly and the incredible design of the Creator expressed in the perfection of its ability to maintain flight with almost no effort. I remember asking the question, "What am I created for?" I knew that after graduating from high school I would move back to the United States for college, but beyond that I had no real sense of direction. Almost immediately I recognized His voice for the first time; I heard Him ask me to give my life to serve Him. My heart leapt and I responded with a definite yes! Looking back, it was not so much a call to ministry as it was a call to lay my life on the altar for Him, a voluntarily lifelong enlistment to fulfill His purposes.

Sometimes we have taken the idea of calling, and applied it only to those who step into some kind of full-time, five-fold ministry. But in reality God has extended His call to every single believer; it comes as an invitation to lay down our life for the sake of the Gospel. Every believer is called to give himself or herself in absolute surrender to the King of Kings so that whatever we do comes out of an awareness of our calling. This means that we need to broaden our understanding of the call of God to encompass the whole of our life.

A CALL TO MINISTRY

When God addressed His people at Mount Sinai, He gave them a corporate identity: *You shall be to Me a kingdom of priests and a holy nation* (Ex 19:6). Before the Levitical Priesthood, God foreordained that His people would all function as priests. This proves He never intended to reserve the priestly ministry for special people. Every one of His people has a special call. The prophet Isaiah reinforces and amplifies this when he prophesied that the time would come when, *you will be called the priests of the Lord, and they shall speak of you as ministers of our God* (Isa 61:6). The Hebrew word used for priest in both passages simply means "serving as a minister." It was not used as a positional word but rather as a functional word. Every believer is called to live their life in such a way that the world around them recognizes them as a minister of God. We are called as priests and ministers.

This idea of the Priesthood of the believer means that every believer should understand God's call to give our lives to love and serve Him. As priests we should expect to have a growing intimate relationship with the Lord Jesus that has a direct influence on every arena of our life. From this place of fellowship, every relationship, every interaction, and every action comes under the influence of our calling. It all starts with saying yes to the call.

When Paul referred to the call of God, he uses the same word for his calling as an apostle and our call as believers. The New Testament does not seem to indicate a special category of call for apostles and a call of lesser importance extended to the rest of the body. The call is the call is the call. We are called to be who we were created to be. If that happens to be an apostle, then be an apostle; if we are called to be a plumber, then be a plumber, carrying His presence and power into that arena. But understand it all flows from one universal call extended to every single believer. We've got to break the mindset that says special people receive a call and the rest don't. The church must come to a place where we understand that every member of the body of Christ has a call to ministry.

Look for a moment at the account of Isaiah's call and commission. Notice carefully the sequence of events: Isaiah is caught up into the presence of God and while there, he hears God asking who will go (Isa 6:8)? Isaiah wasn't called! Isaiah heard Heaven asking, "Who will go?" And Isaiah said, "Me, me, me, me"! All he did was respond to the call that Heaven extended. This global call goes out to every one of us as believers. Isaiah just put up his hand and said, "I'll go." That's the essence of the call of God in our life. It is a continual willingness to say yes to the voice of the Holy Spirit, to daily give ourself to just do it.

Remember when we were kids and our friends were choosing up sides for a game. Those of us who were not very athletic waited on the sidelines thinking, pick me, pick me, hoping not to be the last ones chosen - that's the nature of the call. The call is an invitation to anyone who will say yes. The air around us resonates with the sound of heaven's invitation. Who will say, "Yes, send me"? We really don't have to worry about the specifics of what we are called to, just say "yes." In the act of saying "yes" destiny is released in and through us that has the power to change the whole atmosphere. It changes the way we think. It changes the way we act. Responding to the call of God is about our willingness to say yes.

Oswald Chambers, in his commentary on Isaiah 6:8, writes:

> *God did not direct His call to Isaiah - Isaiah overheard*
> *God saying, 'Who will go for Us?' The call of God is not*

just for a select few but for everyone. Whether I hear God's call or not depends on the condition of my ears, and exactly what I hear depends upon my spiritual attitude.[1]

There is a call going out from heaven and if we will listen like Isaiah did, we will hear that same call. It still rings out today inviting any and every believer to respond. God still looks for somebody who will listen. Which of us will say yes to whatever He asks of us, no matter what it looks like?

A CALL TO ACTION

The initial call of God in our life has very little to do with our ability, but it has everything to do with our willingness to place ourself in obedience to that call. A lot of times we disqualify ourself because we don't think we have the ability to do something, when in truth, He only asks for us to open our heart and place ourselves at His disposal, ready to obey His will. Neither does the call of God initially have anything to do with maturity; it has to do with being willing. All of us were fairly immature when we started out in the work of God, but we weren't called for our maturity, we were called for our willingness.

Although character is important to God, His call on our lives has little to do with character. As we walk in our calling, character gets shaped through our relationship with Him. God chooses us because we said, "Yes, I am available." In later chapters we will discuss how living out the call shapes our character and grows us into maturity. But for this moment, we simply make ourselves available and willing to hear His voice and respond to His invitation.

Invitation to Fellowship

The call of God extends an invitation to enlist as priests and ministers in the expansion of His kingdom. The first component of the call is a priestly function of strengthening our individual relationship with God. Priests were the access point to God, ministering to Him on behalf of the people. Their second responsibility was to turn and minister out to the people. This dual function should always be present in our idea of ministry, remembering that it starts with an upward focus of intimacy. If we do not operate from intimacy, we will never fully fulfill the call of God on our life. We may do some good things, even look successful, but we will never step into the fullness of our destiny because the call to ministry is first and foremost an invitation to intimacy.

Paul tells the Corinthian church that, *God is faithful, through whom you were called into fellowship with His Son, Jesus Christ our Lord* (1 Cor 1:9). We are called first into fellowship. Adam and Eve had perfect fellowship with their Creator, but they lost that fellowship through sin. Now in Christ the starting place of His call on our lives flows out of this restored fellowship. The Greek word (*kleesis*) *called* used here actually means *invitation*. So when God calls, He gives us an invitation to walk in intimate fellowship with Him. But it gets even better! The word *call* comes from the root word for *"welcome"* so we are not just invited in but we are welcomed in. The King of Kings welcomes us into His presence and into partnership with Him.

There is a world of difference between inviting somebody because we feel obligated and inviting someone as a welcomed guest. The call of God has both the invitation and the welcome component. So God's call is not a begrudging invite to a bunch of broken, sinful people. He's not calling us just to put up with us. Not at all! The call of God comes to us as an invitation with a heartfelt welcome. Come belong to something great. Come give our life to something that has value. Come serve something that has eternal consequence. Come invest in something that will have a global impact.

INVITATION TO BELONGING

Walking in our call ushers in that comfortable feeling of belonging. The call is not primarily an emotion; however, when we respond to the invitation we begin to feel like we're home. We feel like we fit; we have found our tribe; we are among our own people. This feeling should permeate us as a church family. Understanding this welcoming component of the call of God on our lives empowers us to live as a welcoming body of believers. We may not be able to reproduce the same level of invitation that He has extended to us but it must be our goal. His open invitation to walk in fellowship with Him carries the implication that we should extend a like invitation to every believer.

Our King has welcomed us into fellowship and we respond to that welcome, not out of an emotion, but from a decision. Many doubt the call of God because they have never felt anything. We don't have to feel something to be invited. In fact, we probably won't feel much until we respond to the welcome. When we choose to align ourselves with the call, we will begin to experience the joy of His presence. So respond now; say yes to His invitation. Simply say yes to making our life available to do His will.

STEP BY STEP

That evening on the hillside when I said yes to God, I didn't see much of His plan for my life. All I knew was that He had asked for something and I gave what I had. I felt sure about going back to the US to get an engineering degree and I felt I would return to Africa. At that time my perfect plan for my life involved buying a Land Rover and trailer filled with every tool known to man. I would then spend my life going from mission station to mission station, fixing stuff. I was born with mechanical aptitude and found identity in my ability to repair most anything - that was the extent of my understanding of the call. All I knew to do was to put my gifts and my ability to fix broken things at His disposal. I simply made the skills He gave me available to God unconditionally; it really wasn't what we imagine as a traditional ministry call. What I did not know at the time was that by responding to His call I had stepped into partnership with the Holy Spirit.

The Call of God:
An Invitation to Partnership

David writes - I believe God has called me into the marketplace ministry. My wife Sandy and I own an auto dealership. I tell others that we are in the "people business," not just the car business. The cars we sell are only a vehicle for sharing the Good News (pun intended). We have dedicated our business to God and He has blessed it, because we seek to put His Kingdom first and operate it in a way that accurately represents and reflects His character. My life's verse is Proverbs 3:5-6. We want this scripture to be practically activated in our business each day as we purchase, then sell our products. We trust in the Lord with all our heart. We do not lean on our own understanding. We acknowledge Him in all our ways. His promise as a result is to direct our decisions.

Our marketing strategy is simple; when we lift up Christ, He draws all men to Himself. Our motto is: "Where our greatest value is always placed on you." I can easily testify about our success in number of units sold, but I would rather share about those who have accepted Christ's salvation, those who have been healed, delivered, or touched by His presence in time of need, or those we have prayed with and seen God work miracles of supernatural provision. We have seen hope restored, people filled with the Holy Spirit and employees discipled. We live for Him and others.

Invitation to Partnership

With the call comes an invitation to partnership with God. When we walk in our calling He redefines our relationship with Him. When we set our hearts to serve Him, He responds with a shift in our identity. Toward the end of Jesus' ministry, He invited His disciples into a new dimension of relationship.

> *No longer do I call you slaves, for the slave does not know what his master is doing; but I have called you friends, for all things that I have heard from My Father I have made known to you* (Jn 15:15).

Responding to God's call for us redefines us as His faithful friends who willingly make ourselves available for whatever purpose He desires.

Boy, that takes all the pressure off, because our primary call is not to perform, but to follow as His loyal friend. If we end up on a platform, fair enough; if we don't, fair enough. It does not matter because our goal is not the platform; it's being His friend and partner. The call functions from a place of intimate companionship. It comes as an invitation to be who He created us to be, a faithful friend. The call then transforms our identity. It shifts us away from this kind of ethereal feeling that at sometime, one day we will really fulfill the call of God. No we won't, unless we do it today, right now, and then tomorrow, and the next day, and the next day, and the next day. No matter how long we have been doing this, there is still for each of us an obligation to daily obedience as His friend and partner in ministry.

Sally and I stumbled into pastoring a church. I don't even think we wanted to do it. After graduation from college, I worked jobs that were mostly to do with my skills, hoping to make enough money to pay off our school loans. At some point a friend told us about a pastor who had just left his little church and he asked us to fill the pulpit till they could find someone. We thought it couldn't hurt anything to go preach a couple of times. So we went down and preached for a few weeks and before we knew it they had called us as their pastors. We thought, okay, I guess we can do this. We never saw a blinding light or heard an audible voice saying, "This is your call." All we had were available hearts combined with a willingness to do whatever He set in front of us. All we knew was to obey the voice of the Holy Spirit with as much grace and love as possible.

The call of God then has little to do with flashing lights or with a "one day I will be" sentiment. *We will never be unless we are now.* We will never get to the goal of our destiny without responding to the call now. The call of God is for every believer and it begins in the next moment with an obedience to respond correctly to the next person in front of us. The next step we take is the obedience that ushers us toward the ultimate vision.

It is the will that responds to the call, meaning that the response does not come from an emotion or even a want to. It is instead a deliberate, even at times, reluctant choice. Jesus told a story in Matthew 21:28 about a brother that said he'd do something, but then didn't follow through. His brother's initial response on the other hand was no, but later he made the decision to do what his father had asked of him. Jesus asked His disciples, "Which one obeyed?" It was not the one that responded from emotion or desire to please, but the one that did what he was asked.

His response said I'm going to follow through even if I don't feel like it. The call of God requires us to give our life to Him even if we don't have an experience like somebody else. Even if we don't ever shake, rattle and roll or do the stuff we see other people doing. We make a choice to obey His call whatever the cost. It gives us the starting point for fulfilling our destiny.

GROWING TOGETHER

When we respond to the call we don't start out mature; but if we hang around the presence of God, we can't help but grow up. If we accept the invitation, we will grow because when we see Him we are changed into that image of the One who created us. So many try to get mature before getting called, instead of responding to the call so that we can mature. Peter told the believers to ...*be all the more diligent to make certain about His calling and choosing you; for as long as you practice these things, you will never stumble* (2 Pet 1:10).

Because the call of God requires a practice of obedience, daily surrender, and daily availability, we are promised that if we step fully into the call, we don't have to stumble. That's what it says. It doesn't say we will probably not stumble; it says never. We are convinced that if we surrender to the call of God, we will never stumble. We are also convinced that oftentimes we stumble either because we have not surrendered to the call, or because we are trying to model our call off somebody else's. When we long to be shaped like some other ministry, it means we have not fully embraced who God has created us to be with a day-by-day surrender of our life.

The call of God provides the context for the development of our character. We are created to function as mature sons or daughters, not as hirelings. We were created to understand the identity that comes from His presence and then allow it to shape our life. Our greatest distress with the religious education today is that we train

14

people to be hirelings in churches, instead of teaching them to hear and obey the call of God. We can't do ministry as a hireling and we can't truly function in any job without a call. It simply becomes a job where we work our way through situations to promotion and to some measure of success in our life. Is that what life is about?

No longer can we just bide our time waiting to see what happens next. God wants to change the way we see the world around us. If we don't have a clear call, our character gets shaped by our environment rather than through our relationship of obedience to Christ. Too many of us are being formed by the environment of our workplace rather than by the formation that comes from intimacy with Him.

AN INVITATION TO VOCATION

The call of God influences us in such a powerful way that even our work life is transformed from simply employment into real spiritual opportunity. Tim Keller expresses it this way:

> *A job is a vocation only if someone else calls you to do it for them rather than for yourself. And so our work can be a calling only if it is reimagined as a mission of service to something beyond merely our own interests.[2]*

Let's look at a couple of words in his definition that are vitally important; first, the distinction between job and vocation. If we look up vocation in the dictionary, we find it defined as a strong feeling of being suitable for a career or occupation. There is a difference between a job and a vocation. On a job, we are just making enough to meet the bills. A vocation on the other hand is when we know God has put us in this position for His glory. This metamorphosis doesn't just happen because we decided it should happen. It happens because we begin to understand that we are positioned in our employment as a result of the call of God on our life. Hear the difference between job and vocation. We may do exactly the same things, but we can choose either to do them as a job or to do them as a vocation.

Doing our work as a vocation changes our attitudes to all we do. We realize that every aspect of our work is worthy of real dedication. How do we get that in our workplace? We get it when we understand that what we are doing, the duties we perform, are done as ones called of God, not simply as employees going through the motions. The call of God should influence every facet of life, everything we do, everything we face, everything we walk in - every part should be done as a response to the call of God. Maturity comes when we begin to understand that no moment of our life can we afford to be lived out from under the call.

Sally and I used to get fussed at because when we would go on vacations, we always had God encounters. People would remind us that we just needed rest! But we ask ourselves, how can you rest from the call? If the call is our life, no matter where we are, we will have God encounters; that is part of being called. Yes, we take days off and sometimes go to nice places, but we still have God encounters, because He called us. Stop fighting the call and say yes to all He has planned for us.

INVITED INTO GRACE

The call of God on our life does not depend on how well we have done so far; it is solely based on His grace. Neither does fulfilling our call rely on our works, likes, wants or even desires. Our call is to His purpose. It is His purpose extended to us in grace based on Christ's sacrifice. Paul explains this to Timothy telling him that

God, has saved us, and called us with a holy calling, not according to our works, but according to His own purpose and grace which was granted us in Christ Jesus from all eternity (2 Tim 1:9).

Because the call originates in grace, living out the call of God in our life becomes a process of being formed into His image. We don't live fearing disobedience or being afraid we might miss it.

Even when or if we do miss it, His grace covers us so that the moment we turn to Him the call is back in action. Paul told the Roman church that …*the gifts and the calling of God are irrevocable* (Rom 11:29). He specifically states that the Father doesn't repent of giving us our gifts and callings. Sin doesn't nullify the call; it only delays it - meaning that the moment we repent, the invitation remains to step back into our destiny! David was called a man after God's heart. But one day he decided to stay home instead of going out to war with his men. He was not where he was supposed to be. In boredom he finds himself on a rooftop watching Bathsheba bathe. He coveted what he saw and took her for himself, even resorting to killing her husband in the process. He was clearly in sin and disobedience.

When confronted by Nathan the prophet, David repented and made things right with God. How indescribable is the restorative power of God's grace. His forgiveness is so complete that the Father could allow His Son Jesus to be born through the union of David and Bathsheba. If we do not understand the grace of God, we will struggle to walk back into the call after a failure. By any standard of measurement, David messed up his call. But somehow God's grace proves so profound that the moment we repent and return, we are restored to the center of His call for our life. It is beyond our comprehension to understand how God can do that, but He does. And He is ready to do it for every single person because of His grace.

It doesn't matter where we have been, what we have done, what we go through, how bad we've messed up, or how terribly we've distorted our call. All is covered if we will come back to the cross and repent. In that moment we are made perfectly holy before Him, invited into His presence and back into His call. Now that's good news!

We have heard so many believers bemoan the fact that they messed up and have lost forever the call of God in their life; but that's nonsense. We might have delayed some things; sin can and will delay the call - no question about it. But the moment we repent and come back, God's forgiveness is so profound that we can immediately step back into the perfect will of God. What an awesome God! How good is He? How merciful is He? How loving is He? How forgiving is He? How powerful is the blood of Jesus to wipe out the sin and restore us back to His original intention!

The Call of God
An Invitation to Surrender

Chuck writes – I have been in business for twenty years as an Agricultural Retailer and Crop Duster. When I surrendered my life to Jesus fourteen years ago I felt pressure to sell everything to follow Jesus. But in the last few years my mindset changed by reading the Word and being mentored by my Pastor and other members in our church. I realized I don't have to sell everything to follow Jesus. I need to put Jesus first in everything, including our business. God is the real owner of this business and He wants it to be prosperous and provide for the people involved, but He also wants to bless our customers and others through this business.

Acting on the urging of the Holy Spirit, we pray for people and have seen a marriage restored, tumors disappear, pain leave, and legs grow out, all for the glory of God. He is so good. Carol and I have staked out the four corners of our property. We placed scriptures in metal cylinders and pounded them into the ground as a physical act of claiming and designating our land for His Kingdom. God has opened my eyes to the fact that I am in a mission field in my area. There are people just as lost, just as hurting as there are in India, Africa, and Brazil right in my own backyard. As my Pastor says, the last great move of God is the saints – you and me – doing the ministry. Let's get up and GO! Your mission field is wherever you are right now!

AN INVITATION TO SURRENDER

The call of God is an invitation to surrender. There is a cost to discipleship that requires a full surrender of our will, our desires, our plans, and our purposes. Full surrender means we say yes to God, unconditionally laying down our life. Surrender means that we choose to do what He wants for us and lay down our right to decide what we want to do. Surrender happens in a moment, followed by a series of moments where we lay our will at the foot of the cross and tell Him, we are Yours, use us. Jesus described this kind of surrender when He said, *whoever does not carry his own cross and come after Me cannot be My disciple* (Lk 14:27). The cost of discipleship is real but the joy of obedience far exceeds any price we could ever pay. With everything in us we long to fulfill the call on our lives and become all He has destined for us. We made the decision long ago to pay the price, whatever the costs.

ARE YOU CALLED?

A friend set up Sally and me on our first date. We went to the same church and we knew each other by name but apart from that we had very little interaction. One afternoon as I walked down the hall in our local church with the youth pastor, he stuck his head into the library where Sally was working and informed her that, "There is a guy out here who's too embarrassed to invite you to the sweet-heart banquet next weekend." We were both shocked! It was the first either of us had heard about it and even though we knew he was joking, we sheepishly agreed. Sally wrote me a nice note the next day letting me know that we really didn't have to go through with it, but we decided to do it. Well, it was a prank that backfired.

Somewhere in accepting the call of God on my life I had made the decision that I shouldn't even date a girl unless she had a clear call to the mission field. I didn't understand then what we do now about the importance of both husband and wife being surrendered to the call, but I know the decision to be careful kept me out of trouble. I had spent some time with a couple of girls who caught my attention but when I asked them if they felt the call of God on their lives I got some interesting responses and it went no further.

That night I sat across from Sally at the banquet and asked my question. "Are you called to the mission field?" She gave me a strange look and asked why I wanted to know. I fumbled a bit and said I just really wanted to know. Then she proceeded to tell me that as a child she had felt called as a missionary and then just a few months before she felt God tell her the time had come to get ready. So in obedience to the call, she had gone down to part time on her job to enable her to go back to school and finish a degree in preparation to go either to China or to Africa. The banquet was in February and we married that August.

We studied together the next year to get all the Bible courses we needed for acceptance as missionaries. After we finished college, Sally and I both knew we would need to work for at least a year to try to pay down school loans. Mission boards frown on going to the field carrying debt, so we did our best to deal with it. However, by the end of that year our daughter Rachel was born, we had moved into a larger apartment and found ourselves in just as much debt as we had when we started.

YIELDING OUR WILL

Sometime during that year we went to a concert. Robert Hale and Dean Wilder were singing at the First Baptist church and Sally had always wanted to hear them. Their voices and music were amazing but one of the songs they performed that night had a profound impact on our lives. When they sang the old hymn, "Sweet Will of God" by Naylor Morris, something happened inside of us. God birthed a desire in us to yield our wills to Him at a depth that I personally had never done. We had said yes to His call, but this was different. We felt convicted that He was asking for a more intimate surrender of ourselves to do His will through us.

That night we bought the cassette with that song on it and played it until we wore it out. The impact of the words governed our lives for the next few months as we made the decision to sell all we had and head to the mission field. The words are still stuck in my head.

My stubborn will at last hath yielded
I would be Thine and Thine alone
And this the prayer my lips are bringing
Lord, let in me Thy will be done
Sweet will of God, still fold me closer
Till I am wholly lost in Thee

The yielding of our will and the recognition that the will can often be stubborn became a theme of our lives. We came to understand that He no longer wanted us just to live our lives knowing we were called to Him. Now, He was asking us to let Him live His life through us. Even though at that time we knew little of the work of the Holy Spirit, we did know that He was asking for an absolute surrender to Him for the rest of our lives.

It all came to a head one evening when we sat down and talked over what we were both feeling. We felt trapped by life and we knew that if we kept doing what we were doing we would quite simply never get to Kenya. That night we prayed and made a commitment to God that we would sell everything and go, no matter the cost. We were choosing to let Him have our will, which left us with no answer but yes. At the same time we reminded God that we still had the debt hanging over us but that we refused to let circumstances stop us from immediate obedience to His call on our lives.

The next morning we made a call to the mission headquarters and signed up for their next missionary candidate school, which was just a couple of months away. I went in to work and turned in my notice, while Sally called the local newspaper and published an advertisement for a moving sale the following weekend. We decided to get rid of all the stuff we didn't think we would need. We had drawn a line and were not turning back.

That evening after making the commitment to go, we got a phone call from a friend of my parents who we had only briefly met. Her reason for calling was to find out what was keeping us from the mission field. I told her about the commitment we had made the night before and that we had made plans to move forward. We also told her about the school debt still hanging over our heads. She then asked me to give her the exact amount we owed. It took a few minutes to find it but as soon as I gave her the dollar figure, she promised to put a check in the mail for the full amount. She told us God had put it on her heart to pay our school debt to release us so we could go to Africa. We were stunned!

God had supernaturally paid off thousands of dollars of school loans with one check and we left for candidate school a few weeks later completely debt free. It was a lesson in surrender. Would she have called if we had not made the decision the night before? We will never know for sure, but I suspect not. The decision to surrender opened the door for the supernatural provision of the resources necessary to fulfill the call.

A PRISONER TO THE CALL

One of the ways Paul describes his relationship to his mission is as a prisoner to the call. He says, *I therefore the prisoner of the Lord, entreat you to walk in a manner worthy of the calling with which you have been called* (Eph 4:1). Paul describes himself as captured by the call of God. He felt imprisoned by the call of God with no desire to escape. The call of God is such a powerful guiding force in everything we do once we become its willing prisoner. Prisoner doesn't sound like a great description, especially in a society where we claim we are free, but Paul views the call as so powerful that once we engage in this call it guides every step. We should all be imprisoned to the call of God. Can we relate to that? Can we relate to being imprisoned by the call of God? If we can, it would change how we live.

During candidate school, our mission decided that they were going to switch over to computers for their record keeping (our age is showing). I had just finished my engineering degree and had taken some computer programing. Because I understood what the company was doing and wanting, I started helping answer questions for the staff. Before long I found myself serving as the liaison between the mission and those writing the software. It turned into a lot of fun as we helped our mission move into the computer age.

When we finished the job, the company doing the setup approached me and offered Sally and me more money than we had ever dreamed of to come and work for them. They wanted us to help them do in other companies what we had just done with our mission. They offered a crazy amount of money, and an amazing position with lots of benefits; but we were prisoners of a call. We were prisoners of obedience to the One who paid the price for us and called us to lay down our lives for Him. We have found in our life that many times when we step into a new obedience we receive an attractive offer to go in another direction that comes along to compete with the call. These can be tempting unless we have chosen to surrender our will to the Master.

Laying down our life is not just for missionaries. When Paul tells us he is a prisoner to the call, he invites every believer to become a prisoner to the call of God regardless of our profession. God has placed in our hearts a desire that can only be fulfilled when we choose to walk in obedience to Him. We will never find true fulfillment outside of a life of obedience. But the obedience God requires is incredibly individual because He has uniquely created each of us. As long as we move in obedience, we are doing what He called us to. Obedience to the call should and will release kingdom influence into every profession on earth as long as we move only out of obedience dictated by the call of God.

Jesus asked His disciples a direct question: *Why do you call me 'Lord, Lord,' and do not do what I say?* (Lk 6:46). The call of God requires a response to His Lordship. When we surrender to the Lordship of Christ, we surrender our right to do anything other than what He says. We believe we are entering into a season in the Body of Christ where living under the Lordship of Christ will prove necessary to release the anointings that He wants to send to the earth. If this is true, then don't be surprised if we find ourselves being tested on Lordship issues. Surrendering to the call and obedience to His Lordship comes down to making ourselves available to Him without restriction.

The Call of God
An Invitation to Availability

Wanda writes – As a nursing professional who does in-home health care, I meet depressed, lonely and sick people that need a kind word, soft embrace or a smile to bring light into their lives if only for a few minutes. God rewards me with these individuals to deposit a part of Him in every face I meet. He sends me undercover as a nurse, but when I enter their life I bring Him with me to touch every aspect of their physical, spiritual and emotional needs. Often I get the opportunity to pray for them and I love how my life with God is integrated into my profession as a nurse.

One day while with a lady who was recovering from surgery, I felt impressed to share a testimony about someone who was healed from deafness. It turned out to be a word of knowledge because – unknown to me – the woman I visited was 80% deaf in her left ear as a result of a childhood infection. She let me pray and as we did she felt her ear pop and she could hear clearly. After we had celebrated, she said, "I don't want to be a prayer hog but could you pray for my knees?" So I told her that I lived under an open heaven and would reach up and get her some new knees. As I prayed, I reached up in the air as if I was grabbing two knees and then placed my hands on her knees. When she checked them out she had greater mobility and was able to bend down and pick things up off the floor, something she had not been able to do in many years. God is so good!

27

BEING AVAILABLE

Brother Andrew, who wrote *God's Smuggler*, once said, "God does not choose people because of their ability but because of their availability."[3] At its most basic, living under His Lordship means making ourselves available to do His will. Availability implies that we avail our ability to Him. The word *avail* means *to be useful or to have value.* So making ourself available means we give whoever we are to Him so that whatever we have is accessible for His use. We want to be useful to Him; so, whatever skills, whatever gifts, whatever time and resources we have, we make available to the Master. That is the nature of surrender, the heart of laying down our life to live under His Lordship. When we pray this, He takes us at our word.

Sometimes we work to become more gifted so we can feel more useful, instead of simply giving all we have to His use. God wants to take who we are right now and shape us into a useful vessel for His kingdom simply because we made ourselves available. The circumstances of our life prove irrelevant when we understand that the mark of His Lordship really comes down to availability. Are we making ourselves available for God to use? This is the decision we all must make because the call is for every believer, in every moment, and at every season. Have we surrendered? Or have we put a list of preconditions on what we are willing to do for Him?

We have found that the more conditions we try to put on the call the less effective we find ourselves. But the reverse is also true, the more we totally surrender, the more effective we become in ministry. None of us walk in effective ministry because we deserve it. We walk in effective service to Him because we have made ourselves available.

We said, God use us to do whatever You need us to do, we just want to be useful to You.

GOING DEEPER

During our preparation for the mission field we were not very good or even comfortable with raising support. But we had made ourselves available and God took us at our word. While attending a conference, God miraculously connected me with Stewart Briscoe, who walked up to me and offered to support us as we went to the field. He and his wife pastored a wonderful growing church that became one of our home bases for several years. Stewart was also one of the main speakers at the Keswick Convention, sometimes known as the Higher Life movement.

The thrust of their message was that believers should move on from his or her initial conversion experience to receive a second work of God. There were various names given to this experience. Some called it entire sanctification, others referred to it as the second blessing, or the second touch, and the brave called it being filled with the Holy Spirit. They taught that Christians who received this blessing from God could live a more consistent Christian life.

We sat under men like Stewart Briscoe, Major Ian Thomas, and Alan Redpath who wouldn't have said they were charismatic, but they introduced us to a deeper work of the Holy Spirit. Their passion was for believers to become Christ-like, first by full surrender to the Lordship of Christ and then by yielding to the work of the Holy Spirit. We learned that if we didn't yield to the Lordship of Christ and surrender to the work of the Holy Spirit, it was doubtful we would ever fulfill our destiny. In hindsight, their teaching that the work of the Holy Spirit was the key to living a normal Christian life set us up for the encounter we had with the Holy Spirit on the mission field years later.

We grew under their teaching and began to break out of some of the limitations of legalism and into a freedom in the Spirit. We came to understand the depth of the call of God and surrendered to Him with a hunger to learn to function the way God created us to function. I remember the day we ran across Major Ian Thomas' definition of spirituality. He said,

> *Spirituality in man is his availability to God for His divine action, and the form of this activity is irrelevant. If it pleases you, always and only, to do what pleases God you can do as you please!*[4]

Read that again several times! This definition impacted us deeply and still today sets the standard in our hearts for spiritual obedience.

Like Brother Andrew, Major Ian Thomas described spirituality in terms of availability to God. But he went a step further; bringing the call of God into every profession and realm of life when he states that the form of spiritual activity is irrelevant. It doesn't matter what job we do or what career we have chosen. The circumstances of our life, background or socioeconomic situation simply don't matter. Spirituality at its core comes down to this - have we made ourselves available?

Forty-five years ago this truth lodged in us. We came to understand that if we choose to always be available, and if we set our hearts to please Him, we are free to live. Jesus fulfilled His call in the same fashion. He said of Himself, *I always do the things that are pleasing to Him* (Jn 8:29). Surrender produces a heart that always seeks to do what pleases Him. How liberating to realize we can do whatever we please with the precondition that we live to please Him. If we want to please Him, we step into a liberty that allows Him to live His life through us. In every arena of our life we can simply function because God has given us the liberty, and we want to live to please Him.

A lot of us are just trying to do what we please and then ask Him to bless what we have chosen to do; but it doesn't work. We keep tripping over ourselves. But if we start with full surrender to His Lordship and a passion to obey Him with everything in us, then the result is incredible liberty. We don't walk around afraid of missing it, because our heart is set to please Him. Because we live to please Him, we will please Him and life becomes full of His pleasure. What incredible liberty. That is why scripture can say, *where the Spirit of the Lord is there is liberty* (2 Cor 3:17), because when the Spirit is in control and we have surrendered to Him, we simply do whatever is in front of us to do. God's call goes out for a body of people who will fully surrender to Him so that they live with a freedom in the Spirit.

TRUE IDENTITY

To fulfill the call on our lives obedience to the Holy Spirit must become our greatest priority. Paul teaches that *...all who are being led by the Spirit of God are the sons of God* (Rom 8:14). This means that our identity as sons and daughters is in some measure tied to our obedience to the Holy Spirit. This should profoundly challenge us. It is possible to have the vocabulary of identity in Christ and yet neglect our relationship with the Holy Spirit. But only when we walk led by the Holy Spirit will we truly walk in the identity He called us to.

So identity is not just a confession of the right truths (yes, please confess the right truths), but our identity actually gets solidified when we walk full of the Holy Spirit. We see a lot of people using the right language but without the power of His presence because they simply are not walking in obedience to the Holy Spirit. This is the heart of hosting His presence. When we walk in fellowship with the Spirit, His presence releases the authority to stand in our position in Him. When we surrender to the Holy Spirit and walk under His Lordship we will begin to walk in our true identity.

The Holy Spirit not only confirms our adoption, He also empowers us to extend the influence of the King. Surrender to the Spirit provides the key to the extension of the Kingdom of God. Jesus said of Himself, *If I by the Spirit of God cast out demons then the Kingdom of God has come among you* (Matt 12:28). Look at the statement He makes without the verb; *If I by the Spirit...then the Kingdom of God.* The Holy Spirit is the operating agent of the Kingdom of God. Whenever we surrender to the Holy Spirit and move in obedience to His promptings, the Kingdom of God is extended and the power of heaven touches earth.

We can add any of the gifts of the Spirit back into the sentence. If we by the Spirit prophesy, then the Kingdom of God has come among us. If we by the Spirit release healing, then the Kingdom of God has come. Any action initiated by the Holy Spirit extends the rule of the King. So whatever you do by the Spirit ushers the Kingdom of God into the environment where we live or work. Every time we release the Spirit we release the Kingdom of God to influence the culture around us. The world needs people who will live so full of the Spirit that they live by the Spirit every moment of their life.

Paul further establishes this principle when he writes to the Romans: *For the Kingdom of God is not eating and drinking but righteousness, peace, and joy in the Holy Spirit* (Rom 14:17). Look again at the active parts of the verse without the verbs. The Kingdom of God is...in the Holy Spirit. *The Kingdom of God is expressed by the Holy Spirit at work in and through the lives of believers.* The more focused we become on hosting His presence; the more we're going to affect and impact the culture around us.

God is calling us to be desperate for more! More surrender to the Holy Spirit, more encounters with Him and more of His life flowing through us into society around us. If we walk in more, we will always sustain a revival culture in our life. It is only when we shift back into our own efforts that we slip out of revival culture and back into the world's system. God help us as churches to break fully out of our self and into full surrender. Make us willing to pay the price to go all the way with You so we can fulfill Your call on our lives.

Harry Linden, an English theologian in the 1830s said it this way: "Nothing is really lost by a life of sacrifice but everything is lost by a failure to obey God's call."[5] There is a call on the life of every one of us that asks for surrender. With that call comes an empowering to do whatever He asks of us. All that remains is for us to yield to the call and live in the freedom that only comes with complete obedience. All He asks for is surrender of our life, making ourself available for His use.

The Call of God
An Invitation to Destiny

Jimmy, a district sales manager for a large tire company writes – One of the keys to fulfilling my calling is to keep my work/home balance in order so I am able to do what I do for the Kingdom. I have many opportunities to share my faith in the workplace but one stands out. Each year one of my key accounts has an annual conference. This dealer has been a part of my business network for nearly 10 years. However the past few years have been an astounding journey and privilege in sharing Christ with them.

Every January this dealer kicks off the year with a four-day event where they lay out all of their policies, prices, and other guidelines that need to be followed. The company knows my beliefs and recognizes that I don't push them on people but simply live my life for Christ every day. Because of this, for the past four years they have asked me to be a minister and motivational speaker for their event. Each of their 600 associates gather on the last day of the conference - Sunday - to hear the Good News of the Gospel in a work environment. For me this is so exciting and rewarding to see them accept Christ and that major tire company leaders would endorse such a thing.

AN INVITATION TO DESTINY

When God calls it's an invitation to step into something. He does not command us to do it; He invites us to do it. He invites us to walk in a partnership with Him more rewarding than anything we've yet experienced; an alliance that leads to the fulfillment of our destiny in Him. The nature of the call is that He invites us into a place of fellowship with Him. He beckons us to go deeper, to go further, to push in. If we accept the priesthood of the believer, then we should have an expectation that every member of the Body of Christ should daily walk in the anointing and presence of the Holy Spirit wherever they go. That should be the normal for us.

Webster defines our calling as a strong inner impulse toward a particular course of action, especially when accompanied by the conviction of divine influence. Thus, anything God puts in our heart to do He sanctifies when we understand that His divine influence is there. So whatever profession, whatever job we do, whatever situation we find ourselves, when we walk with the expectation that God is doing a work through us, it becomes a calling. It's more than just what we do; our employment actually becomes an expression or extension of God's call in our life.

We often use the word "call" exclusively for people who go into some kind of ministry vocation. But we want to kill that religious idea; it's a sacred cow that needs to die. There's no such thing as a secular/sacred distinction under the New Covenant. Every believer works in full-time Christian ministry. Neither is there a clergy/laity divide, where a few elite do the spiritual work and the rest do secular work. Somehow we have to break this idea that has become so ingrained in us. The call of God invites every one of us to step into a destiny with Him, a destiny He has prepared specifically for us.

A Valuable Masterpiece

Paul tells the church that *we are God's workmanship, created in Christ Jesus to do good works, which God prepared in advance for us to do* (Eph 2:10). Some translations substitute the word masterpiece for workmanship. Do we think of ourselves in that way? Take a moment and meditate on the fact that God sees us as His valuable masterpiece. It will change the way we think about things. It will change the way we view the world around us. Do we understand that God created us as a valuable expression of His own workmanship? Paul also points out that there is a direct link between this revelation of our identity and our destiny. Not only did He create us as a valuable work of His hands, but He also prepared something in advance for us to do. God imagined a destiny for us when we were created, and our life's mission is to find it, live in it, and fulfill it.

The four walls of a church building must not limit the role we are to play in His Kingdom. He did not invite us to come to meetings, although they serve as wonderful celebrations of belonging together in the Body of Christ. Our life outside of meetings is just as important as life inside. We are called to do something. We are called to be something. We are called to release something. We are called to express something.

We love being in the atmosphere of corporate worship, but if our spiritual life doesn't carry outside the walls, it really doesn't have the value that God intended. He didn't create us as a valuable masterpiece to sit in a pew and listen to somebody talk. He created us a valuable masterpiece so that He could display us in every part of society, everywhere we go, and everything we do. He wants to display His glory through us and is working in us to change the way we think. It is our responsibility to find what He has called us to do and fulfill it, whatever it is, wherever it is and whatever it looks like.

Ravi Zacharias, an evangelical Christian apologist, wrote,

> *We are all priests before God, there is no such distinction as 'secular or sacred.' In fact, the opposite of sacred is not secular; the opposite of sacred is profane. In short, no follower of Christ does secular work. We all have a sacred calling.[6]*

Thus, everything we do is a sacred work. Our profession is not secular employment but sacred employment because God wants to redefine how we view our work. We want to do our jobs well and with excellence but we've got to break down the idea that our work life is any less sacred or holy than what we do in a meeting.

Imagine the whole of our life as an expression of the valuable masterpiece that He created with His own hands. In simple terms, our destiny is to express His image, which means something has to change in the way we view Christian life. We still have a very meeting-oriented way of thinking; in fact, most Christians have "meetingitis". We have so many meetings that it distorts the way we understand our Christianity. If we hope to fulfill our true calling, it won't happen in a room full of Christians. We can only fulfill it through the way we live the whole of our life.

Enlisted to Full-time

Every believer has a call to full-time ministry. The nature of our profession doesn't matter. Our background is irrelevant. Neither does our skill set, our education or the level of training we have received. Every one of us is called to full-time active Christian ministry. It is our life; the call of God defines us. Sometimes we wait to get fixed before we do what we know He called us to do. But more often than not God wants to heal us and transform us in the act of doing what He's called us to do. He's not interested in waiting years for us to get started; all He asks for is that we say, "I'm ready. I'll do whatever You ask me to do."

When we accepted Christ we gave up the right to opt out of our calling in Him. Even though His call is an invitation, it invites those who have already been purchased by the blood of the Son. Paul says,

> *I have been crucified with Christ; and it is no longer I who live, but Christ lives in me; and the life which I now live in the flesh I live by faith in the Son of God, who loved me and gave Himself up for me* (Gal 2:20).

It is no longer we who live but Christ that lives in us. That means our life does not belong to us. We no longer have the option to focus on our agenda, our desires, our needs, and our wants. If Christ really lives in us, then it's not enough to just live our life knowing that God called us. He actually wants to live His life through us. If we call ourselves a Christian, our life should reflect this call from Christ Himself.

The calling allows Him to live the life through us that He's destined for us. That requires full surrender to the Holy Spirit; it means yielding and daily devotion that asks, "God, what do You want me to do today?" We do not live paranoid, afraid that we might miss it, because there's grace in the call for that. But we do believe that we need to regularly ask God to live through us rather than just going through the motions. Why don't we ask what He wants? If we really were crucified with Christ, if it really is no longer I, then everything we do must be directed at expressing who He is to the world around us.

No matter what job we do, no matter what the circumstance, no matter what situation, we walk into it with the expectancy that God is walking in with us. We walk in knowing that the power of His Holy Spirit is following us. Os Guinness in his book on the call of God describes it this way:

> *If all that a believer does grows out of faith and is done for the glory of God, then all dualistic distinctions are demolished. There is no higher/lower, sacred/secular, perfect/ permitted, contemplative/active or first class/second class. Calling is the premise of Christian existence itself. Calling means that everyone, everywhere and in everything fulfills his or her (secondary) callings in response to God's (primary) calling. For Luther, the peasant and the merchant—for us, the business person, the teacher, the factory worker and the television anchor—can do God's work (or fail to do it) just as much as the minister or missionary.[7]*

Could we actually start believing that? Could the call of God become so strong in our lives that it governs everything that we say, everything we do and everything we are?

If we're called of God, we live that way. If we're called of God, it elevates the way we see the things He gives us to do. It changes the nature of how we feel. Accepting the call means that we choose to view all our personal preferences as secondary to God's call. So, everything we want to do becomes secondary to the primary calling of God. Everything we feel, every gift, every desire, becomes secondary to His primary call on our life.

Paul speaks of himself as being a prisoner to the call. When we surrender to the call, the fellowship we enjoy with our heavenly Father becomes so sweet that once we have tasted His friendship, we don't want to step away from it. As we push deeper into this place of intimacy with Him, the call becomes so strong, so direct, so clear, and so pervasive that it governs every action we take.

Christians who don't want that level of commitment have probably never tasted the joy of His pleasure over us when we live our lives for Him. They want the salvation, the benefits, and they want to avoid hell. But by their actions they communicate, "You've given me eternal life, now just let me live the life I want to live." Unfortunately, that's the way many of us live. Not aware that the moment we received His salvation we were recruited to fulfill His calling. We belong to him, which means that we have a responsibility to fulfill His expectations for His possession.

Speaking of the priesthood of the believer, Luther wrote of the plowman and milkmaid doing the work of God. For us today this extends to every believer in every profession, needing us to recognize that we are just as called as any preacher or missionary. Wow, if we could get that down inside of us. If we could understand that when we walk into our job on Monday morning, we're walking into a spiritual call as much as anybody that ministers from a platform. It's just as important and just as priceless before God. Everything we do in our life needs to anchor in a sense of being called by Him and to Him. Can we allow the Holy Spirit to work that deeply into us?

Paul tells us that *God who is at work in you, both to will and to work for His good pleasure* (Phil 2:13). In other words, when we accept Jesus as our Lord and Savior we surrender our life, making it available to Him to do whatever He requires of us. The nature of the assignment is secondary, all He asks is that we make ourselves available by saying, "Lord I'm Yours, I belong to You, I'm living for Your pleasure."

We believe that in this year believers around the world will begin to respond to the call. It will become so real that we will walk into places and change atmospheres because we understand what He has called us to be and called us to do. We're not just waiting for something else to happen; we're allowing Him to use us to make things happen. We feel like we've lived our whole lives believing for this time. We're stepping into a new season. In place after place, we're seeing people laying down their lives in radical, crazy obedience to the Holy Spirit, believing that He can take us and use us to produce fruit. Get ready.

Prepared for War

In the act of salvation we enlisted with Jesus to live as His disciples and to operate as extensions of the purpose that He walked in here on earth. He came specifically to destroy the works of the evil one; that is the short version of Jesus' purpose statement (1 Jn 3:8). When we received Christ we were recruited to work on His behalf to destroy the works of evil; that's why we're still here. In this spiritual conflict, advancing the kingdom means destroying the works of darkness – sin, sickness, and poverty.

The enemy is a terrorist organization, dedicated to killing, stealing and destroying. God who saved us from the power of the enemy wants to work through us. He transferred us into His kingdom for the express purpose of partnering with Him to destroy the works of darkness. We're here to walk into the shopping mall armed to destroy the works of the evil one, to walk into the post office ready to destroy the works of the evil one. We are to walk into our workplace looking for opportunities to displace the darkness by introducing the kingdom of heaven.

We're created to carry the presence of God wherever we go; that's our destiny, it's what we're called to and it's what we were created for. It doesn't matter whether we understand it or not, or even whether we accept it; that's what He called us to. If we're going to walk in our destiny, we need to step up into what He designed for us and not settle for what we've experienced up until now.

In many ways, the church has moved away from a warfare view of the Kingdom of God and moved into an overemphasis on sovereignty. We believe in the sovereignty of God, but many in the church have embraced a distorted view of the sovereignty of God where we say, "If it happened it must be God's will." From this perspective sickness is inevitable and the decay of our culture is inevitable. We look at the circumstances and feel powerless against all we see happening in a society. But we were created as the answer to that; we were created to have a voice. He created us with a call to bring in the culture of heaven, to demonstrate the heart of our Father, to show the world the grace of God and release His goodness into a society that doesn't understand it or know it. We're created for more than we have walked in.

We must stop accepting things like sickness, which are not from God. God doesn't make His kids sick. It's time we took a stand on this and said, "Not on my watch." As Bill Johnson likes to say, if one of us as parents deliberately made our kid sick just to teach them a lesson, we would be arrested for child abuse. That's not who God is. We need to tackle sickness straight on. We need to attack cancer straight on. We need to confront any work of darkness straight on.

One of the most dramatic transformations we've seen was the healing of a lady with Parkinson's disease. She was wheeled into the first meeting almost comatose. As the power of God touched her, she lifted her head, looked us in the eyes and smiled. The second night she began to move a little more and her face was radiant. When we prayed for her again in the last meeting, she stood up out of her wheelchair. She continues to improve, regaining muscle strength and she has been able to get out of her wheelchair at home and begin to care for herself. We've got to fight these things.

We may not always win, but we've got to fight them. We don't always get the outcome we hoped for; we wish we did. We wish we didn't have to answer the difficult question why. But we know one thing; we've got to stop accepting sickness, because the call of God has recruited us into a militant attack against the works of the enemy. We have got to confront racism. We have got to fight poverty, loneliness and abuse of every kind. We have got to attack the enemy's schemes head on. Loving people requires us to fight for their freedom no matter what is going on around us. That's the call of God; that's our commission. Are we ready for it?

John and Sam Eldredge in their book *Killing Lions* wrote, "One of the great wonders of Christianity is that you were born into your times, to set your times aright."[8] We were born for a purpose; we are not insignificant and it doesn't matter if we don't feel powerful. Every believer has been born into his or her time to bring about reformation. That's the call. We've been born into this moment to bring the presence of God into our sphere of influence. We've been born into this time to release the love of God to people around us. While we don't have control over whether everyone we pray for gets healed, we do have control over whether they feel loved. Our responsibility is to love people and let God testify with us with signs, wonders, miracles, and gifts of the Holy Spirit (Heb 2:4). Our responsibility is that they walk away from an encounter with us having been touched by the love of God they've likely never known, never understood, and never experienced; that's our call.

WORK OF FAITH AND POWER

Paul tells the Thessalonians, ... *we pray for you always that our God may count you worthy of your calling, and fulfill every desire for goodness and the work of faith with power* (2 Thess 1:11). His prayer for them was that they would come to understand that our call comes with the faith and power necessary to do the work. The call of God comes with everything we need to fulfill it. His presence and His power will always accompany us in the act of doing His work. He can't deny Himself, so He's committed. The more aware we are of our call, the more we will naturally host His presence. If we want to learn to host His presence, push into the call. Because the more aware we are of that, the more we begin to walk in it. And we'll see that wherever we go He is there with us in the process.

The eternal perspective of our calling is fulfilled as God displays His goodness to the world through us. He implements His plan through us by equipping us to do His work with His power. His work gets accomplished through us as a direct result of His Holy Spirit at work in us. We only need to respond in faith and obedience to step fully into His destiny for us. So, if we face a challenge in our business, bring Him into it. Ask, "God, we don't know what to do here; we need Your wisdom." When we ask, heaven will speak, releasing the wisdom and resources we need because that's the nature of the call.

Every believer has a destiny and that destiny is to represent the interests of King Jesus here on earth. It does not matter what our job is. It does not matter what background we come from. It does not matter how long it took us to get there. We have one responsibility, to represent King Jesus; that's our destiny.

The Call of God
An Invitation to Intimacy

Kim, a business owner with her husband Walt writes – When I think about the call of God on our lives, I realize how God has taught us more about our faith in Him through running a company than in any other way. Sure, we have had difficulties that have taught us to lean on Him and grow in our love and faith. Despite the challenges, something very special has been happening in the marketplace.

God called us to start our cleaning business to minister to people, specifically single moms. I felt that God's calling on us was to reach people in the 'cleaning world' that would not otherwise be reached. We have ministered to hundreds of people over the years, praying for and encouraging them. We speak life into each person we encounter; sometimes just through a hug with lots of love and other times crying with them, or even doing inner healing and deliverance in the office. We have poured into countless employees financially over the years.

Our office staff that takes care of the phones often find opportunities to minister to both our staff and clients, praying for them or giving a prophetic word. Several have told us that our staff carries the presence of the Lord on them just because they work for us. In the empty buildings at night, we can pray for the people that work there during the day, asking the Lord to release His salvation in that place.

Encountering His Presence

Sally writes, I left my aunt and hurried upstairs to my bedroom in the guesthouse. Sitting in the car that evening with my aunt, she read to me from her well-worn Bible. I realized then that in all the years of my church commitment and service I had never known the depth of meaning that I now sensed. The warmth in the words she read caused emotions to rise. The words brought comfort, but at the same time … conviction.

With no one in the foyer to greet, I hurried to my room and locked the door behind me. I knew I had to pray. Falling to my knees beside the bed, I buried my face in my hands. Over the years I usually knelt to pray, especially before going to bed, but tonight felt very different. The words from the passages my aunt had read and talked with me about swirled around in my head, especially the words from Isaiah 53, for I began to cry out, first in my heart and then aloud, "Forgive me, forgive me, God!"

Kneeling did not feel low enough, so I stretched out on the floor, face down and continued with tears, imploring God to forgive me. I had prayed these same words many times over the years. But this time desperation to know His forgiveness was overwhelming.

Suddenly, as I pleaded in prayer, I became aware of a presence in my room – a presence that filled the room with **holiness**. I wanted to crawl under the carpet but could only cry out with greater intensity to be forgiven.

Through the tears, the heart pain and grief at my sin, I heard my name called. "Sally." Never had I heard my name so beautifully spoken! Ooh! My soul seemed to awaken out of months of darkness and gloom. I sensed His deep love and affection for me, perhaps it was the same compassion expressed by Jesus when He gently spoke Mary Magdalene's name.

As revelation and understanding rushed to my heart and mind, I jumped to my knees, crying out, "Jesus, You died for me!!" In that moment the atmosphere changed as God's love flowed into my room and seemed to intertwine with His Holiness; love and holiness became companions, drawing me into a deeper awareness of His Presence.

CALL TO MISSIONS

From an early age the desire to serve God as a missionary grew strong in me. Each missionary that came to our church and shared about his or her life on the mission field kept the desire stirred – I wondered which it would be, Africa or China. Because I loved caring for people, especially those in hospital care, my Mother encouraged me to become a nurse.

During those teenage years, nursing sounded great; so, I began to prepare myself for entering nursing school, only to find several years later that every door to nursing would be closed because of my partial deafness.

When I was a teenager, Billy Graham came to my hometown. The stadium was packed and I joyously sang in the choir. The message penetrated my heart deeply, compelling me to go forward to give my life fully to Jesus. The follow-up method used in those days was for those who had gone forward to be counseled by the pastor of their church (if they attended a church). I made an appointment with my pastor, the father of one of my best friends, and told him of my incredible experience at the Crusade. He listened, thought for a while, and then told me that I had just had a "mountain top experience and would get over it."

"What!" screamed inside me. I didn't want to get over it; I felt so good. I felt connected to God, really connected. But as the weeks, months, and years went by, I found myself distracted by other things, things that had nothing to do with serving God.

Seven years later, after having made several unholy choices resulting in condemnation, I heard Jesus calling my name and I knew He had forgiven me and made a way for me. I was to walk with Him as my constant companion for the rest of my life - whether as a singer, a teacher or just as a woman who could serve Him – this was my life.

Jesus' Invitation to Follow

At some point in time most all of us have been invited to visit a family member, a friend or perhaps an acquaintance, but few of us have been extended an invitation which had little definition. When Jesus spoke to the men that He called to become His disciples, His invitation was just a simple, "Follow Me." Jesus had invited them to come and abide with Him. Having heard from the Father, He reached out with a call to twelve men and invited them to be His friends. That invitation must have been saturated with love for them to have left what they were doing - all that they knew to do - and follow Him.

As they began their journey with Him, His countenance, His demeanor, His interaction with people must have left them almost breathless. Observing this man, learning from Him and from the things He taught them required total attention and commitment from them. How often did they ask themselves, "What did He mean when He said, 'Follow Me'?"

Jesus introduced them to His Father and demonstrated before them the very nature of God, His Father. What amazing words they had heard from Jesus as He opened their minds and hearts to receive and believe in God, the Father, and personally experience His love for mankind. Mercy, compassion and love flowed from Jesus in their presence as He healed all that came to Him, as He forgave and restored those rejected by the religious. He even brought back to life one of His friends.

So many incredible miracles, so much love, such power and truth – these things and more the disciples saw and experienced in walking with Jesus; and He called them "friends". Jesus sent these, His friends, to accomplish some of the things He had demonstrated to them. Surely their hearts burned with excitement; they were friends, companions of Jesus, gradually becoming more like Him as they walked with Him.

In Him

One day as they walked along, Jesus drew their attention to the vineyards growing in that area. He compared their lives in Him to the fruit-bearing branches on the vine. His purpose was to make them aware of the necessity of nurturing a deep, personal, and uninterrupted relationship with Him. He described it as "abiding" and referred to Himself as the vine and the disciples as branches.

Would this "abiding" mean they were to live with Him, in Him? If so, what did this look like? We use the word abide today to speak of a dwelling place or a place of habitation. In looking at the Greek definition, we find that abide (*meno*) means "to remain, abide, dwell, to persevere".

Could there be any better place to live than in Him? Could there be any safer place? No greater relationship or intimacy could we con-

51

ceive of than dwelling "in Him." To live in Him would mean that we live in all that He is – His nature, His character, His attributes.

Paul, in addressing the Greeks on Mars Hill, mentioned the altar they had built and dedicated to the "Unknown God" and began to introduce this unknown God to them. Paul did exactly what Jesus had done with His disciples; He was making God, His Father, known to them. One day they, too, would answer His call to abide in Him. They would call God their Father because through Jesus they would come to believe and understand that they were the sons (and daughters) of God, and they would understand all the implications of being sons and daughters with the power and authority inherent in that position.

Jesus desires each of us to have the joy, the love, the peace, and so much more that can only be experienced through the intimacy of abiding in Him. We begin to know Him when we abide in Him. The Greek word *know* (*gnosis*) is not an informational or intellectual knowledge of Him but an *understanding, a knowing that comes through experiential* encounters we have with Him. These amazing encounters powerfully connect us to this One who paid the ultimate price for all of mankind. These encounters enable us to know, love, and trust Him in a deep, personal and intimate way.

He spoke to the disciples as they walked past the vineyard, using words heavy with meaning:

> *I am the true vine, and My Father is the vinedresser. Every branch in Me that does not bear fruit, He takes away; and every branch that bears fruit, He prunes it so that it bears more fruit* (Jn 15:1-2).

The disciples knew that these vines were meant to bear fruit - good fruit - and the key, according to Jesus, was to abide in Him.

They had to hear and understand His message about abiding. They had no idea that this relationship would so drastically change their lives.

Branches designed to bear fruit can only do so by abiding in the Source of life, the vine (Him). Jesus further made it clear that those not abiding in the vine would be thrown away as a branch, which would then dry up, be gathered up, thrown into the fire and burned! Wow! That sounds serious! Have we taken these words from the Lord seriously enough?

The Call of God
An Invitation to Abide

Kenny who owns and operates a truck service, repair and performance shop writes - The Word of God states, make your calling and election sure. So many times people fail to realize that God has called them to do a specific job to advance His kingdom in the workplace. He wants our everyday life to be our ministry; it is just as important as being a clergyman. He gives us talents to complete this task; it is up to us to follow His lead and take His presence into the workplace, to bloom where we are planted, to excel in the gifts He has empowered us with. I thank Him daily that He has given me the abilities to solve mechanical issues.

From the beginning I have viewed God as more than a partner in my business; I see Him as the owner. I have been fortunate enough to learn to hear His voice and follow His lead. As I do, He has blessed my business and my family's life to a point that makes us want to strive to do even more for Him. It is such a privilege being a part of and advancing the kingdom of God.

SALLY WRITES ON ABIDING

When we speak of abiding, we usually think of a place in which we have chosen to live and rest, but is it more? What does this "abiding" mean? Do we truly understand it - especially in our culture today with our busy schedules? We know that the Lord was speaking of our relationship with Him and the Father. If the Lord spoke of our inability to bear fruit unless we *abide in Him*, then understanding this phrase is critically important.

Andrew Murray expresses it this way:

> *The branch does not exist for itself, but to bear fruit that can proclaim the excellence of the vine: it has no reason of existence except to be of service to the vine. Glorious image of the calling of the believer, and the entireness of his consecration to the service of his Lord.*[9]

All that we are comes from and belongs to the vine. The abiding relationship with our Lord provides the sole source of our identity and activity.

Jesus also referred to abiding when He asked the question, *Do you not believe that I am in the Father, and the Father is in Me?* (Jn 14:10). This is that abiding place – within Their being. Paul referred to this in his Mars' Hill address, *for in Him we live, and move, and have our being* (Acts 17:28 KJV).

Jesus further explained this relationship by saying, *The words that I say to you I do not speak on My own initiative, but the Father abiding in Me does His works* (Jn 14:10). *Believe Me that I am in the Father, and the Father is in Me; otherwise believe because of the works themselves* (Jn 14:11). This verse verifies the necessity of His abiding in God in order for Him to do the works of His Father; how much more important for us to abide in Him. He even said there would be greater works through us because He was going to the Father and leaving the Holy Spirit with us.

Because we know that Jesus came from the Father, we can imagine Him being in God; but have we truly considered His passionate desire for us to live in Him and operate from that place? Not only does He say that we are to abide in Him, but He states that He abides in us. And by abiding in Him and He in us, will we not be abiding in the very nature of God – Who He is, His character, along with His power and authority? How awesome!!

I believe the current emphasis on the gifts of the Holy Spirit may have overshadowed the importance of the fruit of the Spirit in our lives. Sure, the gifts of the Spirit are important, but without the fruit of the Holy Spirit in evidence, our God is not glorified in the way He should be. There is a foundational understanding of abiding in Him and thus of fruit-bearing that we must enter into in order to bear good fruit, fruit that lasts, fruit that sustains no matter the circumstances. This understanding must have ordered the steps of Jesus – for when people saw Jesus they saw His Father.

ABIDING TODAY

The church today stands at one of the most critical times in history. Up until a few decades ago the values of honor, integrity, and love were evident, even beyond the walls of the church. These values have to do with our character – how we present ourselves to the world. These values are often missing in today's culture – even the value for life itself. In such a time as this the church must set a standard so the world can see Jesus through our lives. And we can only do this by abiding in Him.

Recently, the pursuit of having a naturally supernatural lifestyle has caused many to desire a deeper relationship with Jesus and the Holy Spirit. May every Christian desire this. We must realize that having a life hidden in God gives us access to all of who Jesus is so that the world may see all that He is.

Abiding in Him provides the secret to a fruitful life, a supernatural life, for then we will walk and live more like Jesus did. *Wherever Jesus went there flowed from Him the power, the character, and the very nature of God.* I want that; don't you?

A good place to start in seeking to abide in Him is to remember that He has perfectly made the way for us. His obedience to the Father, His life of miraculous power and authority, and His death and resurrection assures us of this. In asking Jesus to be our Savior and Lord, He lives in us and we in Him! If we have Christ as our Savior, the fruit is in us because the Holy Spirit dwells in us; we just need to activate it.

Quite a few years ago I remember Steve, my husband, making a sound as he sought to portray a tree bearing fruit. He asked the question, "Have you ever heard an apple tree grunting as it tried to bear fruit?" It seemed a funny question, but he went on to say that in actuality many Christians expend quite a lot of time and energy trying to produce the fruit that we already have in us. The fruit of the Holy Spirit will come forth when the desire of our hearts is to fully represent Jesus by abiding in Him, resting in Him, seeking His face and honoring His presence. There is no better life here on earth!

What Does Abiding in Him Mean?

Abiding in Jesus means that we choose to have a constant, intimate, and passionate relationship with Him. Let's look at each of these three descriptions in detail.

Constant relationship – In order to have a constant relationship, we must learn to become aware of His presence at all times. He promised that He would never leave or forsake us, but how easily we forget this in our busy world. We must find our own way of making this relationship of such importance to us that we invite Him into every situation at all times.

Intimate relationship – An intimate relationship is one in which there is nothing hidden and there are no closed doors. Establishing the depth of this relationship will probably take time and persistence. Truly, no relationship of mankind compares to it, for the Lord knows everything about us – past, present, and future. Though we may sense His presence while worshiping in a gathering of people, intimacy with God communicates best privately, where we can clearly hear His voice and know His heart.

Passionate relationship – The very word "passion" reveals the life of Jesus. Whatever Jesus did, He did passionately. God, the Father, so loved the world that He gave His Son; and Jesus' love for mankind required Him to lay down His life for us. I think we can say that King David was a very passionate man. David's intensity and abandonment in his worship of the Lord drew others into worship beyond anything they had previously experienced. His love and zeal for the Lord had him take risks that others would not have considered. He had grown to know the Lord deeply over the years as he lived in the wilderness, tending his earthly father's sheep.

How can we develop this kind of relationship with Him? First, we need to realize that it involves a *cost*. Paul spoke of crucifying the flesh, the self-centered essence of our life before Christ. Our flesh stands in opposition to the purposes of God in our lives. The flesh doesn't give up easily, constantly vying for our attention

At some point (hopefully, early in our Christian lives) we made a decision that flesh would no longer rule in our lives, and we knew we had to be committed in order to keep this decision fully enforced. Paul said, *Now those who belong to Christ Jesus have crucified the flesh with its passions and desires* (Gal 5:24). We must choose to live by this bold declaration: "The flesh is dead!" This decision sets us on a course to *walk by the Spirit* (Gal 5:16).

Developing an intimate, passionate relationship with the Lord also requires us to constantly weed the garden of our mind. Have you ever had a garden that you neglected to give attention to? It is amazing how quickly a beautiful garden can become entangled with weeds that suck the life out of your precious plants.

This weeding does not require us to focus on the negatives; in fact, the very opposite is true. Having crucified the flesh, we now tune our hearts and minds to the voice of the Lord. We stay alert to and aware of the Holy Spirit's presence and communicate with Him throughout the day and often the night. When we see a tiny weed pushing itself into the garden of our hearts, we quickly pluck out the weed and plant the Word of God in its place. This process may be referred to as renewing the mind. Paul says:

> *In reference to your former manner of life, you lay aside the old self, which is being corrupted in accordance with the lusts of deceit, and that you be renewed in the spirit of*

your mind, and put on the new self, which in the likeness of God has been created in righteousness and holiness of the truth. Therefore, laying aside falsehood, speak truth, each one of you with his neighbor, for we are members of one another (Eph 4:22-25).

We can try to grow in Christlikeness through education, attending conferences or reading books, but I believe we all know that maturity in the Lord comes primarily through our intimate relationship with Him – one in which we pursue deeper understanding of His purposes, His character, and His ways. This takes time and a deep desire that pushes other less important things aside.

We are blessed to have the Word of God which clearly and fully reveals the life of Jesus and His dependence on His Father. Again and again Jesus said that He only did what He saw the Father do and would only say what He heard the Father speak." The writer of Hebrews tells us that Jesus ... *is the radiance of His glory and the exact representation of His nature* (Heb 1:3).

Jesus assured the disciples (and us) in John 14:20, *In that day you shall know that I am in My Father and you in Me, and I in you.* What a beautiful assurance we have that the character and nature of God *is in us*! This means that we have the glorious opportunity to reveal God and His nature to the world!

In this same chapter in John, Jesus told us that He would ask the Father to give us another Helper to stay with us FOREVER. That Helper is the Spirit of Truth or the Holy Spirit who will teach us all things. As we earnestly look into the fruit of the Spirit, may our hearts be stirred to desire this fruit – fully mature and ripened. We will grow as we walk in the Spirit and search things out.

When we are at peace with God and man, there is little chance of ugly things coming out of us unexpectedly. What a good place to begin. Are we truly at peace with Him? This can only happen if we have the Prince of Peace as our Savior and Lord. Romans 5:1 speaks of this: *Therefore having been justified by faith, we have peace with God through our Lord Jesus Christ.*

I want us to think on just one of the fruit right now; perhaps one that gets overlooked, the fruit of kindness. The Greek definition intimates that kindness *is the grace which pervades the whole nature, mellowing all which would have been harsh and austere.* Isn't this what is needed here in the world today? The world needs to see a demonstration of true kindness coming from us as believers. Like all the fruit, kindness begins inside of us – in the heart and mind – and then extends outward through our actions as we walk in the Spirit.

I have always loved Micah 6:8, which states, *He has told you, O man, what is good; and what does the Lord require of you but to do justice, to love kindness, and to walk humbly with your God.*

Over the last several years a strong emphasis has emerged of the necessity for us to know who we are in Christ – our identity as sons and daughters of God. Our true identity is a royal identity. What an awesome thought of being part of our Father's royal family and then kneeling to serve someone! With the fruit of the Spirit activated in our lives, our recognition as the sons and daughters of our Father God will be evident.

Developing an intimate relationship with the Lord requires that we crucify the flesh, keep our hearts and minds free of "weeds", and finally, we need to focus on His presence. This is like fertilizing the garden of our mind, and it takes practice. Abiding in Him is not hiding! As we learn to focus on Him, we carry more of His presence into the world, a presence that changes the world around us.

As we recognize and honor the presence of the Holy Spirit while abiding in Him, let us ask Him to awaken the fruit of the Spirit in us and to stir up the desire to manifest His fruit daily. The call of God is a call to abide in Him, to develop an intimate and passionate relationship with Him. This abiding has a cost, but the fruit it produces far outweighs the price we pay. He calls us to focus on His presence and to carry that presence into the world. This call to abide begins in secret, but He calls us to go public with His presence! Take the risk and step out to reveal the nature of our God. How the world needs to see Him!

The Call of God
An Invitation to Community

Vera, an architect in Germany writes – God is especially equipping me in my business. I studied Architecture, to follow the footsteps of my natural father, but on the way, I got lost. I doubted my creativity and was held captive by many lies. Last year when I was about to quit, God led me to a creative conference. The Father did some major work and healing in me, confirming my creativity and restoring my vision and passion! Since then everything has changed.

Recently God led me to partner with a friend and together we have landed two big projects. These are dream jobs, shaped and put together by heaven! It was a miracle we got them, but even better is that I feel appointed to be able to successfully accomplish it as we partner with God. I am discovering authority and skills I have never recognized before. God showed me how He is going to touch people in my country through this work. He is giving me prophetic floor plans, colors, textures and words, which speak into the hearts of the people. Heavenly Architecture will make a deep prophetic impact on people in this time. It will change whole families and cities as His Glory enters into living rooms through His kingdom living here on earth as it is in heaven, homes where families will feel His presence, care, and love for them.

The Call is an Invitation to Community

Earlier this year I had an unusually vivid dream. That night I had gone to bed thinking about and praying for a friend who had badly damaged an eye the day before. In the dream, I saw a cutaway view of the function of an eye. I watched as the eye saw a need and then followed the path of the need as the image passed through the lens where it was focused to land perfectly on the retina. The retina then converted the image into a signal that the optic nerve carried to the brain. The brain registered it, processed the situation and forwarded a request to the heart. The heart okayed the request, sent it back to the brain, which sent a coordinated signal to the hands and feet to reach out and meet the need. No one part could fulfill their function without the others. The interconnectedness of the diverse parts worked together in harmony to produce something of value. This truth in science carries over into our relationships with one another.

The New Testament teaches that the body of Christ functions as an amazingly intricate collection of diverse parts, all designed to function in conjunction with the others. No one part of the body will ever succeed in fulfilling his or her individual calling without the others. We were created incomplete by design. Scripture tells us that, *there is one body and one Spirit, just as also you were called in one hope of your calling* (Eph 4:4). The hope of our calling is rooted in the nature of the body, a body made up of unique parts all designed to function interdependently. No individual part of the body can do its work unless the neighboring parts work in conjunction or unison to make that happen. To fulfill our calling in God we are invited to fit our lives into a community of believers so that together we can fulfill the purposes of God on the earth. The invitation is to function as a community where we love one another, encourage each other, build each other up and bear each other's burdens.

When we spend any time with our brothers and sisters, we quickly realize that they look different; they think and even act differently than we do. But with all their uniqueness, they still fit as part of this one glorious body of Christ. The revelation we need is that this diversity is not a weakness but actually the strength of God's design. It takes our differences for us to accomplish anything together. When we understand that no single part can ever fulfill their purpose on the earth without the others it gives purpose to our unity. When we know we need each other, it motivates us to stay together. So, if our neighbor doesn't think like us, instead of rejecting their perspective, begin by listening so we can learn to see the situation through their eyes.

It doesn't necessarily mean we change, it simply means that we accept each other without condemnation. We accept each other without criticism or anger. Our society is displaying divisions deeper than we have ever known; so, it is time for the church to walk in more unity than we have ever represented. It is time for us to walk together and see the value in each other even if we don't understand their perspective. For those called of God, there is an invitation to live, walk and work in community. The invitation calls on us to value the interconnectedness of the Body of Christ and accept that together we can produce more than any one of us can on our own. The invitation challenges us to protect our unity and choose to walk together.

Sally and I have been married a long time now, and even with over 46 years of practice we still don't always see things the same. Sally sees things through her perspective and gift while I see through mine, which means that if we don't talk through our different perspectives we can get in a mess. Neither one is necessarily wrong; we just see two different facets, and most often the aspect we see takes priority. With our own perspective as the priority, we then tend to think that what we see is truth and thus other perspectives must be wrong. We then stop listening and spend our energies trying to convince others of our perspective. But community always sees more aspects of a situation than an individual will ever see. There are things that other people prioritize that we might not see the same way, but what they see has great value to them. We must be willing to let people have different perspectives and yet still represent Jesus.

CALLED TO FELLOWSHIP

Our first and primary call is into fellowship with the Father. The blood of Jesus opened the way for restored relationship and He invited us in to have regular communion with Him. *God is faithful through whom you are called into fellowship with His Son, Jesus Christ our Lord* (1 Cor 1:9). The call into intimacy and relationship with Jesus is our ultimate priority. We will only walk in the fullness of our call if we walk in vital fellowship with Him. We won't have anything to give to others if it doesn't come out of fellowship with Him. We can't teach unless it flows out of fellowship with Him. We can't truly walk in unity with our brothers and sisters if it doesn't come out of relationship with Him.

Out of our relationship of intimacy with Him we grow in His love, we embrace His joy, and we learn to live in His peace. Paul tells the church that if they experience encouragement in Christ, they will be able to carry it over into the rest of their life. If they are touched by His love, they will find it possible to share His love with others. If they have encounters and fellowship with the Holy Spirit, then maintaining the unity of the Spirit will come naturally to them (Phil 2:1, 2). The fellowship we have with the Godhead has a direct impact on our ability to live in community and maintain living relationships with others.

This truth is borne out when Paul makes a plea to the church immediately following his affirmation of our call to fellowship with the Lord Jesus.

> *Now I exhort you, brethren, by the name of our Lord Jesus Christ, that you all agree and that there be no divisions among you, but that you be made complete in the same mind and in the same judgment* (1 Cor 1:10).

Why is He exhorting us like this? Because we are called to fellowship! The fellowship we maintain with Jesus has a direct affect on our fellowship with each other. The challenge given in the name of the Lord Jesus is for us all to agree, and allow no divisions among us. How do we do that when we appear so different and see things from such different perspectives?

CALLED TO UNITE

Paul's exhortation mirrors Jesus' assertion that the greatest commandment is to love God and love our neighbor. We can't do one without the other. But perhaps more important, the ability to love our neighbor flows directly from our vertical fellowship. Salvation restored our fellowship with Jesus, and the fellowship with Him has a direct effect on our fellowship with one another. **The call of God includes the grace to create an agreement with each other powerful enough to bridge divisions.** Scripture can say with confidence that, *there is neither Jew nor Greek, there is neither slave nor free man, there is neither male nor female; for you are all one in Christ Jesus* (Gal 3:28). The community of those who respond to the call will become living demonstrations that every division created from the fall is now demolished in Christ Jesus. True Christian fellowship will make us one.

69

Early in the life of the New Testament Church, the leadership faced a crisis that forced them to deal with the Jew/Gentile division. In the history of the church, it is hard to imagine an issue more potentially divisive. The fledgling Church was faced with two cultures that constantly clashed. Each culture was supported by contradictory value systems, by contrasting histories, and by a set of beliefs that stood diametrically opposed to the other. The Church at its birth had to learn to overcome one of the greatest divisions in all of church history.

Their solution to this crucial issue was to gather those involved, then stay together to talk and pray until they came out with a stunning agreement. *For it seemed good to the Holy Spirit and to us to lay upon you no greater burden than these essentials* (Acts 15:28). Look at the starting place of the agreement, it originated in their fellowship with and hearing from the Holy Spirit. Once the Holy Spirit had spoken they came into agreement with their vertical relationship and applied it to the challenge in their horizontal relationship. It seems good to the Holy Spirit! We need this both for the church and for our nation at the moment. We need to behave according to *what seems good to the Holy Spirit*. We want to love and act as seems good to the Holy Spirit. We want to walk with such a sense of community that we can bridge the differences that so easily divide. If the church doesn't demonstrate this kind of unity, the world will never have the opportunity to see it.

When Jesus prayed for His disciples and those they would reach down through the years, His request of the Father was that He would equip them to walk in a culture-defying unity, a unity powerful enough that no division would be able to prevail against His church. *I in them and You in Me, that they may be perfected in unity, so that the world may know that You sent Me* (Jn 17:23). The perfected unity of the believer demonstrated in and through the church is what catches the attention of the world. When we as the community of believers choose to walk together - even when division would seem unavoidable - that decision impacts the world allowing them to see the reconciling power of Christ. Be careful in this season, because with division so rampant, we need to pray.

God help us see what You see because we don't see very clearly. Help us to see our brothers and sisters through Your eyes, so we can honor them as You honor them. Help us to learn to accept them just as You accept them even if we don't understand some of their positions. Deliver us from making judgments against them and teach us to live with a passion for reconciliation.

The phrase *perfected in unity* can also be translated, *being perfected into a unit*. We define a unit as a group of individuals coming together to accomplish a task. When we hear this word we think of an emergency unit or a military unit. A unit has a purpose; members are trained and disciplined to respond immediately to needs they encounter. They learn one another's strengths and weaknesses and understand how to react in any given situation. This is true team ministry, recognizing that we desperately need each other, and understanding that only together are we complete. To function as a unit we need the revelation that no matter how gifted we are, God created us incomplete by design.

Sally and I had the privilege of planting and pastoring a primarily African-American church in Atlanta. We had successfully planted a multiracial church in Leeds, England that bridged both the ethnic and socioeconomic divide that existed in the community. But then God asked us to return to the States and do the same in our own roots. It proved challenging, to say the least. It is one thing to help others through their own issues but in this new work, we ourselves became part of the issue. We had to sit down numerous times with some of the leaders and ask them to help us see what they were seeing. We struggled to conceive that some of the positions they held had validity. We needed to hear one another, not because we wanted to challenge what they were seeing, but because we wanted to understand how they got to their position. And even when we agree to disagree, we do it with understanding and compassion.

If we have hearts for unity, God will give us the grace to accept our brothers and sisters who don't see it quite like we do. They are seeing one facet of the heart of God while we are focused on a different facet. Unity comes when we make a decision that we want to see more than just our facet of truth. Community comes because we choose to make ourselves willing to take a risk and genuinely listen to opinions that appear contrary to ours. Then together take that diversity into the presence of God and let Him shine His light of truth on our apparent conflict – only then can we walk in true fellowship with one another.

The Call of God
An Invitation to Fellowship

Paul, a special education teacher writes - After getting baptized in the Holy Spirit in high school during the Brownsville revival, I felt God calling me to go to Bible College. But after graduating with a BA in pastoral ministry, I did not feel led to pursue a job in full-time vocational ministry. However, God did open the door for me to become a special education teacher for students with emotional/behavioral disabilities. I learned more about the heart of the Father there than I could've anywhere else. After many years of teaching in that environment, God opened the door for me to become a special education teacher at the elementary school two blocks from my home church.

My wife and I were asked to become part-time children's pastors at our church about a year later. God has called us and opened the doors for us to pastor and care for the children of our neighborhood, both churched and unchurched, and has given us the influence and favor to do so. When I walk into work every morning, I am able to affect the lives of over 200 students for 8 hours, and in turn, have an open door to engage their families with the presence and power of the Holy Spirit.

CALLED TO FELLOWSHIP

Walking in the light of His presence will create fellowship, ... *if we walk in the Light as He Himself is in the Light, we have fellowship with one another, and the blood of Jesus His Son cleanses us from all sin* (1 Jn 1:7). The focus is on Him and His purpose, not on our earthly perspective. Can we understand that sometimes our perspective is wrong? Sometimes it is not even our perspective; often we just need to deal with our reaction to somebody else's perspective. God wants to bring us into a fellowship with one another that displays to the world that people who are different can still walk together.

Historically, when the Holy Spirit has been poured out, His presence has bridged the gap between people from diverse backgrounds. In fact, a distinguishing mark of a legitimate outpouring has been the power to draw people together. A prime example was the revival at Azusa Street. William Seymour believed that the color line was washed away in the blood, and his faith in the truth of the Word was richly rewarded with a stunning breakthrough in the racial divide in one of the most fragmented periods of our nation. Even though the church never really grasped the truth of what had taken place, we believe the move of the Spirit we are now experiencing will have that same power to unite.

CALLED TO LOVE

Christian community begins with a decision to love. Jesus gave *a new commandment... that you love one another, even as I have loved you, that you also love one another* (Jn 13:34). The decision to love is a human impossibility unless we access His kind of love. To consistently respond with unconditional love we must individually deal with the intrinsic selfishness of our nature. John tells us that *we love because He first loved us* (1 Jn 4:19). This verse accurately describes our human capacity to love; we are responders. In our humanity we find it easy to respond to what others say or do and have little intrinsic ability to initiate love. This makes accessing God's kind of love an essential component for sustaining a spiritual community.

In contrast, God loved us while we were still sinners (Rom 5:8). His love is not influenced by or dependent on our responses. His love always initiates the correct response, despite the circumstances. When we operate out of His love we can love those who have no ability to love us back. We can love those that the world has discarded. But sometimes even more difficult, we can begin to love the body of Christ despite our differences. We can love our neighbor no matter what he or she says or does to us. We can love those who gossip and spread evil reports about us.

In the natural realm this feels impossible, but Paul assures us that *the love of God has been poured out within our hearts through the Holy Spirit* (Rom 5:5). The Holy Spirit makes an unlimited supply of God's initiating love available to us, simply by asking. Community depends on our commitment to access God's love in our walk with others. It also requires that we use our gifts to serve one another, trusting that in the process we will receive the love and input we need to fulfill our calling.

To do this, we need to make a commitment to wear the love of God like a garment. *Beyond all these things put on love, which is the perfect bond of unity* (Col 3:14). This means we have a choice to prepare ourselves to consistently love. In fact, a mark of spiritual maturity is fostering a lifestyle in which we learn to love as Jesus loved. He promised that if we practice this central aspect of life together in community, then peace will rule among us.

The glory of this truth is that it doesn't stop with the community. The ripple effect of our love for each other becomes the distinctive that attracts the world to the truth. *By this all men will know that you are My disciples, if you have love for one another* (Jn 13:35). His love, expressed through us, will not only be the distinguishing mark of our community, it will prove so attractive that it serves as a calling card for salvation.

CALLED TO ENCOURAGE

Another cornerstone in our invitation to community is the call to encourage. The writer of Hebrews exhorts us:

> *...consider how to stimulate one another to love and good deeds, not forsaking our own assembling together, as is the habit of some, but encouraging one another; and all the more as you see the day drawing near* (Heb 10:24-25).

This injunction gives the activity of our love for one another. It is not enough to have an attitude of love; God's love has actions. Our interactions with each other should be marked by encouragement that comes from deliberate forethought. This suggests more than accidently giving encouragement; it requires that we "consider," think and imagine ways to stir our brothers and sisters to live out their faith.

The phrase "one another" used here occurs numerous times in the New Testament and appears to cover most areas of life and relationship. The references to one another give us a glimpse into the breadth of what it means to live in the encouraging atmosphere of a community. This fellowship of believers includes confession of sins one to another (Jas 5:16); it calls on us to be kind to one another (Eph 4:32) and to live at peace with each other (1 Thess 5:13). When we fellowship we build each other up (1 Thess 5:11) and when necessary we comfort one another (1 Thess 4:18). If anyone does something against us, we must forgive that person (Eph 4:32). Fellowship requires that we worship together (Eph 5:19) and spend time praying for one another (Jas 5:16).

We are called to be devoted to one another (Rom 12:10) and to honor one another (Rom 12:10). Scripture calls on us to live in harmony with one another (1 Pet 3:8), meaning that we must accept one another (Rom 15:7). As we work together we serve one another in love (Gal 5:13) and make sure that we are always kind, gentle and compassionate to one another (Eph 4:32). We also must learn to admonish one another (Col 3:16) in such a way that it does not take away from the command to encourage one another (Heb 3:13). To move forward we must consciously spur one another on toward love and good deeds (Heb 10:24). We are commanded to love one another (1 Pet 1:22) and to offer others hospitality (1 Pet 4:9). Then add to that contributing to the needs of the saints (Rom 12:13) and bearing with those who are weak (Rom 14:1), we then get a glimpse into what true community should look like!

The body of Christ desperately needs the encouragers to rise up. Barnabas, whose name means son of encouragement, was the perfect model who gave his life and ministry to being an encourager. Each of us needs others to surround us with their love, support, prayer, and ideas, as well as their gifts so that we can fulfill all God has called us to do. This encouragement has the power to strengthen us to serve others.

CALLED TO STRENGTHEN

Any relationships within community will only grow as strong as our willingness to think of the needs of the other person and make it a priority and to act to meet those needs. When we focus on ourselves we are not really together. But when we live to meet the needs of our brothers and sisters we will all grow stronger and will discover a new depth of relationship. The scriptural injunction for this aspect of community is to *bear one another's burdens, and thereby fulfill the law of Christ* (Gal 6:2). Clearly, God expects us to give ourselves to strengthening one another. Just as Jesus gave Himself to serve and not to be served, we are asked to live by His example. It is the law of Christ.

This responsibility to help each other means that we can never isolate ourselves from other believers. If we do, then how can we possibly help them in their time of need? The reverse also proves true: How can we expect to receive all we need if we have chosen to reject the community portion of our calling? Not only is it attractive to see the body of Christ working together as one, but also we are stronger and more like Christ together than when we stand alone. When we walk with a high value for our brothers and sisters, we will begin to realize how crucial community is to fulfilling our calling.

Paul makes this clear to the Ephesians when he wrote,

> *but speaking the truth in love, we are to grow up in all aspects into Him who is the head, even Christ, from whom the whole body, being fitted and held together by what every joint supplies, according to the proper working of each individual part, causes the growth of the body for the building up of itself in love* (Eph 4:15-16).

The body of Christ needs community to grow and develop into maturity. Every part supplies something necessary for the individual parts to grow and for the whole to reach the goal. The call on our lives includes this invitation to community, where together we love one another, encourage each other, build each other up and bear one another's burdens.

Discerning the Body

In the Last Supper Jesus did and said some incredible things. He instructed us to continue to take communion together as an ordinance where we could remember what He did and said until He returns. As well as an act of remembering, it is also a celebration of restoration and healing.

He first took the bread and broke it as a representation of His body that was broken for us. His body that went through torment so that we could have freedom and healing. But the bread also represented His spiritual Body, the church. As we break bread together there is healing for the brokenness in the Body of Christ. We are healed when we make a commitment to walk with our brothers and sisters even when we don't understand them. We make a commitment to love despite what they do. When we take the bread together we are making a commitment to live in community.

One of the strongest warnings in scripture is the caution against eating the bread and the cup in an unworthy manner. Historically the church has taken this primarily to refer to sin in our life. Though that has merit, the context is actually referring to having something against our brother and sister. The text tells us that if we eat the bread with a bad heart toward our brother or sister we have not understood what's in the bread. We have not fully understood that His body was broken so that we could be made whole. So, next time we take the bread, let us examine our heart. If there is any anger or frustration at a brother or sister, deal with it so that we can together steward the unity of the body.

The world is desperate to see what they haven't yet seen. Since the early church, the body has not functioned in a true unity. The unity needed is a unity of the Spirit where the body so tunes itself to the Holy Spirit that we behave as a single unit. This is what we live for as we watch the body of Christ awakening around the earth. We live to see the church step into the unity that the world needs to see. A body that displays His power, yes, but displays it from a united heart. The power for this transformation is in the bread and the cup.

Then He took the cup, the ultimate symbol of surrender. It was His blood. His precious blood did more than just forgive us and cleanse us from sin. His blood has the power to transform us, changing us into His image. Let's make a commitment to Him and to each other that we will give ourselves to learning what it means to be perfected in unity.

10

The Call of God
An Invitation to Intercession

Melissa writes, A little over a year ago, I was homebound with an incurable, debilitating disease. The Lord healed me, and today I work at a private Christian school as the music teacher. Just by showing up to work every day, I'm a testimony to the miraculous power of God. Everyone remembers the events I missed due to illness. Though I often feel restricted by the reformed theology the school embraces, I've been able to serve the Lord, the school and its families in several ways.

Each morning, I pray over the classroom I work in and the campus as a whole, asking for blessing, favor and protection. In addition to practical service and assistance, I encourage, prophesy over and pray for the teacher I work with almost every day. We've seen God answer those prayers time and again. God shows me things about the children, which I pray into. One of the children who has been dismissed as "difficult," sneaks me a smile from time to time. She knows I love her. Actually, I have a thing for the "difficult" ones. They're my favorites. I've also prayed for several children with ailments and have seen many of them healed.

One teacher suffered a concussion at the beginning of the school year. One day, I overheard her talking about ongoing symptoms. I prayed for her in the presence of the wives of the Headmaster and the Director of the Board of the school. She came to me the next day, thanked me for praying and told me with tears in her eyes that God had healed her. She hasn't had any problems since.

Sally Writes on Intercession

One of the most exciting parts of the call on our lives involves growing a deep, intimate relationship with the Lord. When Jesus demonstrated prayer to His disciples, it seemed as though He reached out His hand to them and said, "Come with Me into a life of adventure. As My Father directs by His Spirit, your partnering with Me in praying and standing in the gap will see many lives changed, transformed. The great harvest to be gathered requires your intercession with Mine in order to bring them into the fold."

I had been a Christian many years when I first heard the term intercession. Up until that time I had addressed the Father in prayer, making requests or even pleading with Him often and on many occasions, but what did intercession mean? While on the mission field with my husband we were filled with the Holy Spirit, and praying in tongues gloriously changed my prayer life. When we held prayer meetings for local pastors in the large living room of our old colonial home in Kenya, as many as 50 pastors would gather and cry out for revival.

On one occasion I found a tract left behind (written in English); it seemed to call my name. It related the weapons of warfare listed in 2 Cor 10:3-6 to intercession. "What?" I had read the verse many times but never really applied it to my prayer life. The tract discussed ways to pray and intercede and made it sound very powerful! (I wish I had that tract now.)

My pursuit turned toward intercession. At that time in Kenya I attended many prayer meetings but questioned if they really understood the kind of intercession referred to in that tract. Not long after starting the pursuit, God relocated us to Northern England. I remember thinking, "Maybe this is where I am to learn about intercession."

THE COST OF INTERCESSION

In talking to the staff of the training center's dormitory where we lived at the time, one of the dorm parents loaned me a book which he said would teach me all about intercession. In reading the book, *Rees Howells, Intercessor*, it seemed a bolt of lightning hit me. This story portrayed a deeply committed life of prayer, communication with the Father, and a discipline I had never walked out. Before fully completing it, I laid it aside. A part of the story troubled me. Rees Howells and his wife went to Africa without their child, leaving him with trusted friends. "No," I thought, "the price of intercession exceeds anything I had imagined – it's too high!"

Little did I know that I had already started the training to intercede. Cost? Suddenly thoughts of Jesus came to me - Jesus, the Mediator between God and man. Could His life have been that of an intercessor?

Jesus gave instructions to His disciples when He left them in the Garden and went off on His own to pray – costly prayer. They prayed, but not as Jesus had requested. He instructed them to ... *keep watch with Me* (Matt 26:38) and to *pray that you may not enter into temptation* (Lk 22:40).

Something had taken place in my heart, and in the reading of Howells' biography my desire to live as an intercessor came alive. I realized that my life was to be impregnated with prayer – early in the mornings, sometimes late into the nights, deep cries from my heart. *Compelled* would best describe my prayer life, especially in times of difficulty. My prayer times were intimate, powerful, and life-changing. I had begun the training and I loved it.

What am I Seeing?

Some of those prayer times deeply affected me; one of them had to do with a vision. On occasion I would be praying and realize that I was seeing a woman in my mind's eyes. During the middle of the night I would wake and see this same woman's face. Middle-aged, short, humbly dressed with a scarf on her head, this woman's weathered face showed weariness and worry. Off and on for years her face would appear to me; I would pray for her each time, sometimes only in my heavenly language. It turned into a memorable experience.

After many years of praying for her, my husband and I were in Mexico with a team. I had spoken at a women's meeting at one of the churches and gave an invitation for salvation. The translator and I had prayed for several ladies and then seeing that the next lady in line was very short, I knelt in front of her and lifted her face. To my astonishment, it was the lady from the vision!! I was so excited I could hardly speak. After the service we found that she was from an unreached Indian tribe in the mountains that the church had been praying for. Years before, God had invited me to intercede for this woman and her tribe, and that day I felt like I saw the first fruits of my prayers. We never know what glorious opportunity the Lord will bring to us if we just follow His lead.

Interceding for a City

A large part of the Holy Spirit's training took place in the inner city of Leeds, England. This assignment from God was everything Steve and I wanted and felt we were born for. I was interceding daily and sometimes with fairly large groups; we cried out for His love to spread across the city, replacing the hatred and bringing reconciliation. A multiracial church soon came into being.

Eleven years later God sent us to the inner city of Atlanta, Georgia, where we put into practice what He had been teaching us about intercession. Though we felt displaced – having been absent from the United States for 18 years – God used our prayers and leadership to help birth a thriving, primarily African-American church, now several thousand members strong. It was another inner city church birthed in intercession.

After a brief time in Oklahoma, God directed us to plant a church in Springfield, Missouri, a small city with very little racial diversity. As we sought to break through the strongholds over the city, our intercession became more and more focused and passionate. Through intercession we have watched God close nearby drug houses, birth a church in revival and change the atmosphere of our city. I believe that, as God's children, *wanting to learn* qualifies us to become His disciples. But to fulfill our calling we also need to learn some of these keys to intercession.

I have been awed by the intimate relationship we can have with God through intercession. We are incredibly blessed that the Father has provided two intercessors for us: Jesus Christ and the Holy Spirit.

JESUS OUR INTERCESSOR

Jesus Christ was sent by the Father to represent God to mankind and, through His death and resurrection, reconciled man to God. Isaiah states, ...*For He bore the sin of many and made intercession for the trans-*

gressors (Isa 53:12 NIV). The cross represents the gap between God and man that could be bridged no other way than by the innocent blood of Jesus, our Savior, Intercessor, and Mediator. While in France last year, I saw a painting of Christ on the cross as the Father would have seen Him from heaven; it impacted me greatly. The Great Intercessor had truly bridged the gap at great cost to Himself and the Father.

Today Jesus our High Priest sits at the right hand of God, interceding for us. ...*He is able to save them to the uttermost that come unto God by Him, seeing He ever lives to make intercession for them* (Heb 7:25). Jesus continually makes intercession for us and through us, but He is also our Advocate. ...*And if any one sins, we have an advocate with the Father, Jesus Christ, the righteous* (1 Jn 2:1). He speaks to the Father on our behalf.

THE INDWELLING INTERCESSOR

Jesus informed His disciples of the Helper to come (Jn 14:16). He spoke of the Holy Spirit as the "Spirit of truth", the "counselor" or "comforter". This same Holy Spirit also acts as our indwelling intercessor.

> *In the same way the Spirit also helps our weakness; for we do not know how to pray as we should, but the Spirit Himself intercedes for us with groanings too deep for words; and He who searches the hearts knows what the mind of the Spirit is, because He intercedes for the saints according to the will of God* (Rom 8:26, 27).

I am sure that at times we have experienced a burden of intercession from the Lord so deep that only groans came from us, but the Father who gave us the prayer burden understood fully. The distinguishing mark of the work of intercession by the Holy Spirit is that He intercedes *through* the believer whom He indwells. We are the vessels through which the prayer of faith proceeds as we submit to Him.

CALL TO INTERCESSION

The Old Testament is filled with examples of intercessors. Abraham interceded for his nephew and family who lived in the wicked city of Sodom, saving them from disaster. A primary part of the life of Moses was standing in the gap as intercessor for His people, the Israelites. But we, His Church, must come to understand our need to come before Him in prayer, intercession on behalf of the things He commands of us. It is in intercession that we overcome the enemy who tries to thwart the call on our lives as children of God.

Scripture makes it clear where the real battle is:

If My people, who are called by My name, humble themselves and pray and seek My face and turn from their wicked ways, then I will hear from heaven, and will forgive their sin and will heal their land (2 Chron 7:14).

This prayer, required by God, changes lives; it changes cities and changes nations. Spirit-directed, fervent, penetrating prayer combined with triumphant faith brings breakthrough to release destiny and to cause justice to flow down like a river.

God called for intercessors through His prophet Ezekiel.

And I searched for a man among them who should build up the wall and stand in the gap before Me for the land, that I should not destroy it; but I found no one (Ez 22:30).

How sad! How many places may have been destroyed because no one was found to intercede? We have His Word; we can hear His voice and yet destruction continues today. Paul Billheimer wrote,

> *The Church, through her resurrection and ascension with Christ, is already legally on the throne. Through the use of her weapons of prayer and faith she holds in this present throbbing moment the balance of power in world affairs.* [10]

Many religions beg and plead, hoping to gain acceptance from their gods. We, however, are privileged to have fellowship with our God and even partner with Him in His mission.

THE WEAPONS OF OUR WARFARE

The passage of scripture that awakened me to intercession gives great insight into our mission as intercessors. We are first told through the passage that we do not *war according to the flesh* (2 Cor 10:3-6). War? Yes, principalities and powers war against the Spirit of God and His people, and we are called to engage in this war through intercession, not through fleshly warring. Our weapons are divinely powerful for the destruction of fortresses.

Instead of banging away at these principalities and powers with little or no heavenly direction, Paul informs us that we must ready ourselves in order to be the instruments of breakthrough God intends us to be. We must begin by dealing with speculations (human or otherwise) and dealing with every lofty thing that would raise itself up against the knowledge of God (i.e. the religious spirit or the political spirit) - anything that would distort our perception of God (2 Cor 10:5).

Paul goes on to say that we must take *every thought captive to the obedience of Christ*. Our thoughts cannot take off in some random or ungodly direction; they must be submitted to Christ. I believe that doing this enables us to hear the Holy Spirit more clearly, with our hearts and minds cleansed of wrong and harmful thoughts and attitudes. Now let's look at our authority in this war.

AUTHORITY

Redeemed mankind must learn to use the authority that has been restored to us through the death, resurrection and ascension of Christ. We, the Church, the Bride of Christ must carry out the victory that has been won. Through the name of Jesus, we have the authority to resist and overcome the enemy who holds the lost world in bondage and seeks to tempt us all into sin.

In these days in which we live, we see so much wrongly used authority; it may cause some to want to run. God will soon change this reaction if we, as His children, will submit ourselves to Him and His ways and do only what He commands us to do. Paul reminds us that ... *in Him all the fullness of Deity dwells in bodily form, and in Him you have been made complete, and He is the head over all rule and authority* (Col 2:9,10). All authority in the universe has been given to Jesus, and He delegates to us the authority we need to do His work. Paul then says,

> *When you were dead in your transgressions and the uncir-*
> *cumcision of your flesh, He made you alive together with*
> *Him, having forgiven us all our transgressions, having*
> *canceled out the certificate of debt consisting of decrees*
> *against us, which was hostile to us; and He has taken it*
> *out of the way, having nailed it to the cross. When He*

*had disarmed the rulers and authorities, He made a pub-
lic display of them, having triumphed over them through
Him* (Col 2:13-15).

In these days we **must** understand the authority that has been
restored to us. We must see the necessity of this authority! When
we are under authority (having submitted to authority), we can
then operate in greater authority (Matt 8:5-13).

The victory is complete, nothing lacking; we are set free to be
victorious in the work of the Lord. As we intercede, we participate
in His victory, even if we do not immediately see the results. What
joy this brings to intercessors; we don't have to live under a heavy
burden but can enter into His joy!

Sphere of Authority

God stated His original intention from the very beginning:

> *God created man in His own image, in the image of
> God He created him; male and female He created them.
> God blessed them; and God said to them, 'Be fruitful
> and multiply, and fill the earth, and subdue it; and rule
> over the fish of the sea and over the birds of the sky and
> over every living thing that moves on the earth* (Gen
> 1:26-28).

Adam and Eve were created to represent God *to the whole of
creation*. God gave them and their descendants the responsibility
for governing the whole earth. On the day we were created, God
appointed us as intercessors or mediators on behalf of the earth and
all that is in it. Notice that God used the word "subdue" in their

commission. This word is always used in the sense of putting down something that would try to take over.

As we know, when Adam and Eve sinned, the dominion they had been given was stolen by another - Satan. God's plan through the incarnation was to free us from sin and restore our rule or dominion of the earth (Isa 53:10,11; 2 Cor 5:21; Heb 4:15). Through the perfect and complete work of Christ, mankind was redeemed from the curse of our sin and our dominion was restored. The complete and perfect work of Christ cancelled every claim of Satan because, with every legal requirement completed, dominion or rule was placed back into the hands of mankind. **And we must not forget that because of the victory of Christ, Satan and his demons have no authority outside of what mankind gives to him through lives of disobedience.**

Through the name of Jesus, the Church has the authority to resist and overcome the very one who had drawn Adam and Eve into sin and caused them to be cast from the Garden. Now the Church must learn to reign in this life in order to reign with the Father eternally (Rom 5:17-21, Rev 2:26; 3:21; 1 Cor 6:2-3). Our mission is for our believing, triumphant faith to bind and cast the enemy out of situations and places. The Church, through prayer, is to implement the decisions, **the will of God** in the affairs of the earth.

In the return of this dominion to mankind several stipulations were placed on the right to rule. The first is submission and surrender to Jesus as Lord of our lives, which means we seek His direction, hear His voice, and follow His lead.

Then one of the crucial ones is that we are to operate according to measure of rule. Paul states, *But we will not boast beyond our measure, but within the measure of the sphere which God apportioned to us as a measure, to reach even as far as you* (2 Cor 10:13). Paul referred to himself as an apostle to the Gentiles, whereas he referred to Peter as an apostle to the Jews. Measure in this passage refers to territory, but it could also refer to faith or to gifts. Paul alludes to this when he speaks of the grace given to him, and how *God has allotted to each a measure of faith* (Rom 12:3).

God has chosen that areas, spheres, and territories are important. So we see territory and faith as being significant in order to rule, all according to the allotment of grace, and *according to the proper working of each individual part* (Eph 4:16). When a person begins to step beyond their measure, they may struggle, get stuck, or encounter something they had not prepared for. A policeman only has authority to make arrests in his own city; a Kansas City policeman could not ticket a speeder in Chicago. Knowing this should not bring fear, instead only the knowledge that we are to be led by the Holy Spirit of God in all we do.

We stated previously that measure, territory, or sphere is very important to God. In creation, He very carefully measured everything (Isa 40:12; Hab 3:6) and He allotted specific land to His chosen people. Paul was given areas over which he had been given authority to exercise his leadership gifts. We each are given a sphere of function in which our gifts will be used, a role to fulfill within that sphere, and a calling.

THE BATTLE AND THE ARMOR

Paul says to ...*be strong in the Lord and the power of His might, and to put on the full armor of God, so that you will be able to stand firm against the schemes of the devil.* This is a full-scale war, but God has fully provided for our victory. Paul goes on to say:

> *For our struggle is not against flesh and blood, but against*

the rulers, against the powers, against the world forces of this darkness, against the spiritual forces of wickedness in the heavenly places (Eph 6:12).

In dealing with such rulers, powers and forces we understand why we must destroy the wrong mindsets, speculations, everything that would get in the way of hearing the Spirit directing our battle. Paul continues, *Therefore, take up the full armor of God, so that you will be able to resist in the evil day, and having done everything, to stand firm* (Eph 6:13). We arm ourselves with every provision of the Lord and **stand,** waiting for His further instructions. Here we truly must recognize the **importance** of submission to our Lord. We must depend on the Holy Spirit to lead and guide us into all truth and into the way in which to walk (3 Jn 3) so that we can, being led by Him, accomplish all that God intends.

THE CALL – AN INVITATION

We have an invitation from the Father, by the Son, through the Holy Spirit to intercede, to stand in the gap between heaven and earth on behalf of what the Father directs us to bring before Him in intercession. This invitation is like no other because of Who extended the invitation and because of the breadth of this invitation. Truly, intercession is one aspect of this glorious call. Join me and countless thousands in becoming part of God's "on the ground forces" commissioned to see the Kingdom of God extended and the end-time harvest brought in.

The Call of God
An Invitation to Encounter

*Greg an engineer for a large oil company in South Africa writes –
When my wife and I first considered going on a Brazil trip we felt like
we were stepping off a cliff. We had only seen one or two minor healings
and so we had visions of everyone else being used and we would be left
standing. Having said that, we wanted to put ourselves in a place where
we were fully dependent on God, and trust that this time would leave us
forever changed. When we arrived what struck me first was that almost
everyone we prayed for the first night was healed. The church we were in
was so full of faith.*

*While we were in Brazil we had two profound encounters with the
Holy Spirit. In the first experience I was overcome with laughter - something I had never experienced before - and in the second encounter, I wept
over the brokenness of my country. Since we arrived home we have been
so encouraged at the way the Holy Spirit continues to move through us.
We have seen healings and salvations in the church, in the hospital, in
the townships and even at work. We have seen so much of God's goodness,
and too much of God's healing power to ever be satisfied with the way we
used to live! There has been no greater thrill, nothing more exhilarating
than to see God meet people lovingly and powerfully in their place of need.*

AN INVITATION TO ENCOUNTER

When God calls us, He calls us unto Himself. As we have seen earlier, the word "call" carries the idea of an invitation into a loving relationship with Him that grows steadily deeper and more intimate. The call on our life is also an invitation to encounters with the Holy Spirit. The Spirit wants to touch us with the power of His presence that launches us out into effective ministry to others. We need to raise our level of expectation that God has encounters available that we have not sought or even imagined. There are encounters available for every believer. When we encounter the presence of God in a powerful way, it is easy to say "yes" to anything He asks of us. Let's make a decision to say yes, knowing He wants to touch us and encounter us. There is more!

Having been raised in fairly stoic Christianity, we had little expectation that there was more than we had experienced. In our Baptist days, we understood the need to surrender to the Lordship of Christ, but after that initial experience we just gritted our teeth, gutted it out and proved we could do it. Then we got touched by the Holy Spirit and experienced an encounter of the power, presence and overwhelming love of the Father. We saw firsthand that an encounter with His presence changes everything. It infused us with the love of God; it altered the way we looked at the world around us and it adjusted the way we viewed people. We want every believer, called by God, to respond to His invitation to have encounter after encounter with Him.

All of us are called, so every one of us needs to expect encounters with the Spirit of God that wreck us permanently. As we do we will come to realize that encounters are intended to be more available than we've understood. There are special times when we get specific impartations, but we need to live with anticipation of even more than we have experienced. We believe we should be looking for multiple encounters in our lifetime that radically shift our perspective and break us out of complacency.

Encounters are a divine jump-start, an immersion in His power and love that propel us into our calling. Encounters with the Spirit touch us with the power of His presence in such a dynamic way that it launches us out into effective ministry for others. When we encounter the presence of God in a powerful way, it becomes easy to say "yes" to anything He asks of us.

OF FAITH AND POWER

To lay a scriptural foundation for this, look at Paul's prayer for the church to fulfill her calling. ...*We pray for you always that our God may count you worthy of your calling, and fulfill every desire for goodness and the work of faith with power* (2 Thess 1:11). He began with a request for us to live worthy of our calling. We must see the value in obedience to the call to be found worthy, but we also need to understand heaven's perspective of living worthy. There is an eternal perspective part of our call. We are called to spend our life doing things that affect eternity instead of focusing on the here and now. The "yes" we give when we respond to His call requires us to live from heaven's perspective, not just from our temporal understanding. We are called to renew our mind so we think like citizens of the kingdom of God.

Paul goes on to describe what that looks like. The secret to being found worthy is to live our lives so full of faith and power that we display the goodness of God to those we encounter. God's intention is to infuse those He calls with the desire to see the world touched and transformed by the power of His great salvation. He wants to infuse in us a passion for everyone to experience how good this God really is; that's the heart of His call. Then, out of that desire to see His goodness displayed, we learn to do the work of faith and power that causes it to happen.

The calling always includes this element: the goodness of God displayed through us, as we by faith release His power and glory into the earth. We demonstrate His goodness by the way we live our lives. Through our encounters with Him, He plants in us the desire to display His goodness to the world. Our calling is then implemented through the work of faith with power. The call of God comes with the power available to do His work; we only need to respond in faith and obedience. This applies to every one of us no matter what our vocation.

Because the call is to display the goodness of God, it is more an attitude of heart surrender than a call to a particular occupation. This is not just for pastors and missionaries. We can function as a plumber, baker or office worker who fleshes out the goodness of God with lives of faith and power in the act of doing our job. Each of us can operate in as much of our calling as we are willing to say yes to. The call to display His goodness works in every job, business or vocation.

The calling comes complete with all the resources necessary to do what He called us to do. The moment we respond to the call, everything we need is made available to fulfill that call, whether it is spiritual, financial, or material. Peter assured us

> *...that His divine power has granted to us everything*
> *pertaining to life and godliness, through the true knowl-*

*edge of Him who called us by His own glory and excel-
lence* (2 Pet 1:3).

His calling comes with all the resources necessary to complete the task. As an automatic part of His call on our lives, He makes a commitment to equip us. Obedience to the call is our response to Him; the empowering encounter is His reply, filling and equipping us for ministry. The revelation of our access to His resources comes through our identity as His sons and daughters and by abiding in His presence, always hungry for more.

THERE IS MORE

We see this pattern of encounters in the book of Acts. The disciples had spent time with Jesus, observing and participating in His life of power. When He left, He instructed them not to leave Jerusalem until they had their own encounter. In obedience, they wait in the upper room until the feast of Pentecost. In a moment, they are baptized in the outpouring of the Holy Spirit. What a wonderful, amazing encounter, accompanied with wind, fire, tongues, and boldness. They came down out of the upper room empowered to change the world.

It was an incredible encounter, but we often view it as an isolated historical event. We miss the fact that two chapters later it happens again. Peter and John, freshly out of prison, return to the house where the church has gathered. After everybody celebrates, they began praying for more boldness, more of what got them imprisoned in the first place. As they cried out for boldness and a greater release of signs and wonders, the house where they were meeting was shaken *and they were all filled with the Holy Ghost, and they spoke the word of God with boldness* (Acts 4:31). Boldness landed Peter and John in prison, but as soon as they ask for more, they had another encounter and were all filled with the Spirit and boldness.

Some of the same people who were filled in the first encounter are now filled again. How do we miss that? In the next chapter, Peter is back in prison and an angel came to escort him out, another supernatural encounter (Acts 5). Within the first few references to the early church Peter has had at least three divine encounters, not to mention the healing and other miracles he had seen. We suggest that we should live with the expectation that if we're operating in the call of God, supernatural encounters will become the norm to us. Why should we anticipate anything less? We need divine encounters in order to participate with God in what He wants to do on the earth today. Why not expect to be touched and filled by the Holy Spirit again and again and again.

The word *filled means to infuse, to saturate, and to bring under the influence.* That makes sense of Paul's statement to the Ephesian church, *and do not get drunk with wine, for that is dissipation, but be filled with the Spirit* (Eph. 5:18). When we are under the influence of the Holy Spirit, we should not be surprised if there are outward manifestations of this inward infusion. Our human bodies can respond in some unusual ways when infused with the power and presence of the living God.

As those called of God, we must learn to live under the influence of His Spirit. We can't survive with occasional visits with the Holy Spirit. We've got to live each day under the influence of the Spirit, so infused by the Spirit of God that we walk out of our times in worship carrying His presence. When we respond to the call we should expect a filling of the Spirit. Not just hope that one day we might have an encounter, but actually anticipating that the Holy Spirit wants to touch us regularly and take us deeper than we've ever gone before.

THE ENCOUNTER

Encounters with the Holy Spirit sensitize us to the spiritual realm. His presence and power tune our ears to hear His voice and awakens our minds to understand His Word. The love of the Father flowing into us touches our hearts, delivering us from fear and intimidation. He anoints us for ministry and fills our hearts with compassion so we can see the needs around us. In His presence, we hear the truth of how He sees us, which establishes our identity as His sons and daughters. Encounters with Him move us out of the limitations of the natural mind and into a renewed mind where the supernatural becomes normal.

The more encounters we have, the more spiritually aware we become. Through encounters with the Holy Spirit, God opens our eyes to the unseen realm. He wants us to see what He sees, hear what He hears and speak what He speaks. Encounters orient us to the supernatural. They usher us into the spiritual realm so we can see things, hear things and do things that we never could before. Our perspective of the world around us changes; we no longer look at our circumstances with uncertainty or fear; we see life from a position of the victory of our King. We live aware of the Kingdom and see it advancing and taking ground despite opposition.

Through encounters with Him, our eyes lift off of the world around us and fix on His victory. We live to see His Kingdom come, and we desire to see life only through His eyes. We become harvest focused, recognizing that the wheat is growing, ripening and already starting to come in. What we see happening in the Kingdom becomes our focus so we live overwhelmed by His goodness and excited about the future. While we do recognize that tares are maturing as well, we refuse to let our agenda be set by what the enemy is doing on the earth; we want it set only by what the King is doing. We choose to live fully vested in what God is doing, a decision that gives us an optimistic and eternal view of life.

DIVERSITY OF DESIGN

In the natural, we have desires, skills and gifts that God will use in our pursuit of the call, but there's more. He wants to work through us with a greater release of His power and presence that only comes through encounters with His Spirit. We can't sustain the passion in our calling without more of His love, His grace, and His mercy. God designed us to be vessels who live full of His presence, and as such, we should expect continuous filling with His Spirit.

Because each of us is different, the encounters we experience will be diverse. There is not necessarily any significant difference between shaking under His power and weeping quietly in a corner. The secret is obedience to His voice and fully yielding to His Spirit no matter the outward manifestation. It would be a mistake to assume that we should experience exactly what someone else experienced. Just because we have not had an encounter as strong as the one someone else has does not mean ours is any less dynamic. We should not measure ours against theirs or theirs against ours.

Sally and I have had very different experiences but both are equally valid. Her initial experience of the baptism of the Spirit was much more dramatic than my quiet receiving of the truth. And while

I have had times of being overwhelmed by the presence of God, we have had to carry Sally to the car more than once. One night at a small group meeting in a farmer's house Sally got totally blasted, and was on the floor unable to get up. When the time came to go home, she was still out of it and our host came up the basement stairs with a wheelbarrow to get her to the car. We all lost it after that. When we finally got her home, she shook, laughed and cried all night long. It was a life-transforming encounter.

Paul's Encounter

Paul's encounter on the road to Damascus transformed him into a different man. He was on the way to persecute Christians when he encountered the risen Lord Jesus. A voice and the blinding light interrupted him mid-journey and wrecked his plan. His life changed, his perspective altered, and he was left dazed and blind. He waited in a house sightless for three days until finally Ananias came on a direct commission from the Holy Spirit to lay hands on him. When he did, Saul was filled with the Holy Spirit, his name was changed to Paul and he was given a new calling. He became a ...*chosen instrument to take the Gospel to the Gentiles* (Acts 9:15). To complete the encounter, as Ananias laid hands on him, scales fell from his eyes, restoring his physical sight but also empowering him to see into the spiritual realm.

The transformation Paul experienced in some measure remains available to us. We need to stay hungry and even desperate for more of the presence and power of the Holy Spirit. The person of the Holy Spirit comes as a gift from a loving Father. His promise to us was, *If you then, being evil, know how to give good gifts to your children, how much more will your heavenly Father give the Holy Spirit to those who ask Him* (Lk 11:13). We're really good about using that verse when we're referring to the baptism in the Holy Spirit. When we use it, we're thinking in terms of a single encounter, an event where we receive a package of gifts. But we act like that single event is enough to sustain us for the rest of our lives. We want to suggest that this verse was never intended to describe one encounter, because some of the people He spoke to had more than one encounter with the Holy Spirit. God wants us to live with that expectancy of more.

Every September or October Sally and I go to Brazil with Randy Clark just for us. We go to soak in the revival presence we experience there and watch God do amazing things; we go because we need the encounter. We need to see it to carry it. We stay hungry for fresh encounters in the presence of the Lord. As we see Him working extraordinary miracles, we grow an expectation that they will happen through us on a regular basis. Something has to shift our normal and the best way to shift our normal is regular encounters with the Holy Spirit. We believe God is going to encounter us in ways that we've not understood or expected. He wants to do more in and through us than we can even imagine.

So often in Christianity, we have an idea that once we have had an experience we don't need to revisit it. We had an experience of laughter and we went through that season but we assume the season has passed. What happened to living in joy? The season of laughter was to teach us abiding joy. The season was not just an experience; the season was the reintroduction of a kingdom value into the body. But these experiences when we are touched by joy are not just about joy – they are teaching us the value of the encounter.

Look at what Luke says about encounters: *Therefore repent and return, so that your sins may be wiped away, in order that times of refreshing may come from the presence of the Lord* (Acts 3:19). This verse is generally used to emphasize the need for repentance, and rightly so. We need to repent if we are participating in sin. But the key truth for us here is that refreshing doesn't come from repentance; refreshing comes from presence. Refreshing comes because we spend time in the presence of God. When we get in the presence of God we may want to repent, but the benefit of presence is refreshing.

The word *refreshing* actually describes the act of cooling off after a hot day. Remember being overheated and the relief we feel when we get to a place where we can cool off; that's refreshing. The word also means, *to relieve like a cool breeze.* Something happens in the presence that's more than spiritual; He actually wants to touch our body and soul as well - meaning that our mind, will, emotions and even our physical body can be affected when we encounter the presence of God. David said of the Lord, "He restores my soul."

The word *refreshing* comes from a root meaning, *to get our breath back.* If we've ever had the wind knocked out of us, we will remember the relief when we could breathe again. We have all tried to see how long we could hold our breath and remember the desperation building in our lungs to take a breath. Refreshing is that feeling of relief that comes when we can breathe again; that's the essence of the times of refreshing that come from the presence of God.

If we can't get that next breath, something really bad is going to happen to us; that's the kind of desperation we need for His presence. So desperate for the touch of His Spirit that we feel like we must have that next breath to live. When we respond to His call we position ourselves for an encounter with His Spirit because His call includes a standing invitation to refreshing in His Presence. God extends to each of us a welcome invitation into presence so we can get our breath back.

The Call of God
An Invitation to Abundance

Matt writes – As a contractor responsible for multiple projects in various areas of the country, I can get pressed down and tired. One morning I was complaining to the Lord, insisting that my time would be better spent doing ministry full time instead of being stuck behind a desk. I love bringing finances into the kingdom, but I felt disconnected from my destiny, stuck in the middle of what felt unimportant.

That day I was writing two large checks to bless ministries. One was to a national Sozo training ministry and the other to a Human Trafficking task force. While signing them I felt to pray for these seeds to multiply. Suddenly Holy Spirit came on me in my office in such power I couldn't catch my breath. As I signed the Sozo check Holy Spirit spoke saying, "This is you partnering with Me as I roar against lies the enemy has told about Me". I literally began to roar loudly in the spirit. The same thing happened when I signed the other check. Holy Spirit said, "This is you partnering with Me as I roar against injustice". I had the same roaring experience, which was wonderful and alarming at the same time.

Now my posture when I work is to see my value in the kingdom, and that ministry is a lifestyle of encounter. God also taught me that a grace that I couldn't see was attached to that check to go and do what it was sent for. I found out that both ministries received a mighty influx of finance after receiving our check. Grace was multiplied.

Invitation to Abundance

God wants to stretch us in the area of our belief about His ability to release abundance to us and through us. Most of us have spiritual and denominational histories that have created some confusion about financial prosperity. We have heard of or seen some excesses, but the call of God requires us to shake off our concerns, hesitations, and uncertainties about what someone else has done. It is time to ask God to help us understand how to live in His abundance because we need a release in this area, both individually and corporately. We aren't going to accomplish all we're called to do with either a poverty mindset or an entitlement mindset. We must break off these mindsets and embrace God's promise of more, a realm of abundance where we have access to provision that we don't yet understand. As we will see in this chapter, the promise of abundant blessing applies to anyone who will say yes to Him.

Most promises in scripture have an obedience clause, and many of them are tied directly to our call. Paul speaks from experience connecting one of these promises to the call of God on his life, and by implication to ours. *And we know that God causes all things to work together for good to those who love God, to those who are called according to His purpose* (Rom 8:28). Obedience to the call of God comes with promises of effectiveness. The principle here is that when we walk in obedience to the call and purpose of God, then everything that happens to us works to the ultimate fulfillment of His purpose and plan. If we love God and operate in His call, then all things work together for good.

God is inviting us to partner with Him in effective ministry; He simply asks us to respond to His invitation. When we do, He orchestrates every situation we face so that it advances His kingdom. Paul says of his own calling, *my circumstances have been turned for the greater progress of the Gospel* (Phil 1:12). Every circumstance he ever faced, both positive and negative, ended up advancing the Gospel. When we apply this, there is no circumstance we face that cannot be turned to release the full blessing of His purpose and plan for us. God wants to shift something in us so we come to expect to live in His blessing. Living a blessed life shifts the way we think, the way we act, and the way we interact, resulting in an abundance mindset.

BREAKING OUT OF POVERTY

Breaking out of poverty and into abundance is available within the call of God. One of Paul's prayers for the church was for us to awaken to the glory of the inheritance available to us. *I pray that the eyes of your heart may be enlightened, so that you may know what is the hope of His calling, what are the riches of the glory of His inheritance* (Eph 1:18). We usually move this to the future, instead of recognizing it as a promise connected to the call on our life. God is beyond time, so when He gives us a promise concerning His inheritance it will at least in part apply to us today. As sons and daughters of the King, there is an inheritance that we walk in now. And while we recognize that the fullness of the promise is still future, there is more of our inheritance that we need to access today. All God asks is that we accept the promise of abundance and position ourselves to receive. He wants to do something extraordinary in and through us, releasing all the finance and resources we need, whatever that looks like. God wants to instill this truth into us, but first, something has to shift in our thinking for us to take hold of it.

I grew up in a fundamentalist, cessationist household. My parents' negative view of the Charismatic Movement meant they assumed that anyone who spoke in tongues was demon possessed. When I finally came into the fullness of the Holy Spirit, we joined a group of believers very resistant to the idea of prosperity in the Gospel. Add to that some of our own experiences with "name it and claim it" church members we pastored, and we were left with little good to say about the movement. But we are so thankful that God did not allow us to stay there.

It all changed on a mission trip to the Island of Dominica in the mid-80s. I had gone to help a local pastor set up a small furniture factory to serve as his means of income. What I didn't know until I arrived was that I had also been scheduled as a co-speaker in a conference with Myles Munroe (can you say setup?). Before the meetings started I had to go out and buy some dress clothes just to fit in. After the first meeting, I had to deal with a judgmental heart attitude toward him and what he represented. By His grace, the things God put on my heart to share and the things that God had given to him actually meshed well.

Toward the end of the conference, we had a free day and Myles - along with his camera crew and entourage - decided they would tour the island. Dominica is one of the few places where there were still villages of Carib Indians and he wanted to go and meet some of the original Caribbeans. We set off in a van together and had driven maybe ten or fifteen miles when he told the driver to stop. We pulled off the highway and Myles got out and walked up to a woman who was standing at the side of the road and asked her when she had her surgery. As it turned out, she was just walking home from the hospital and experiencing a lot of pain. Myles laid hands on her, prayed for her, and instantly the pain left. Then after giving her a little money from his pocket to help her cover medical bills, he got back in the van and we drove off. Ok, that was pretty cool.

Then a short while later, he told his driver, "Turn in here." We pulled into a little dirt track that led up to a small village of five or six houses. Myles got out of the van, and I followed close behind (by now I was curious). He walked straight into one of the homes (he didn't even knock) and asked, "Where's the woman that's sick?" They took him to the back bedroom where a woman lay in bed seriously ill. He laid hands on her and instantly she got gloriously healed. He then brought her out to the courtyard where the rest of the group had been waiting.

Myles talked with the family for a few minutes and then asked why the kids weren't in school. They explained that they could not go because they had no money to buy the required school uniforms. He then took off his cap and passed it around to all of us. As soon as he had the money, he walked the twenty-five yards down to the main road where we had turned in. Almost the moment he got to the main road, the van that circled the island selling uniforms pulled up in front of him. Myles bought uniforms for all of the kids and then we got back in our van and went on to the next and the next encounter.

After the experience in that little Carib village, I was a blubbering idiot. Myles had access to an abundance that I didn't even know existed. He walked in a blessing I did not understand and had no reference point to find. That night I did a lot of repenting and soul searching, and the first thing the next morning before we all left, I asked him to lay hands on me. I desperately needed an impartation of the power, faith, and boldness I had witnessed the day before. I want to suggest that if we're going to fulfill our calling as believers, we're all going to have to walk into a season of unprecedented abundance. We will need to break any entitlement mindset or poverty mindset that still hangs on to us. We must step into the fullness of all God has available. Abundance comes when we understand the need to prioritize our life around the call.

Setting Our Priority

A few years ago God asked me to walk an obedience that had to do with setting our priorities. I was reading Jesus' promise to His disciples that if they would seek first the kingdom of God then all of their needs would be supplied (Matt 6:33). It's an incredible promise of provision. If we will put His Kingdom first, then He literally provides everything needed to fulfill our calling. He becomes responsible for resourcing what He calls us to do; that is absolutely liberating. When we begin to walk in heaven's provision, it changes the way we look at problems, circumstances or situations we face.

What the Lord spoke to me was this: **If our need is our priority, then our ability is our source; but if the kingdom is our priority, then the King becomes our source.**

This is the shift in thinking that God wants for us in the church. Instead of His people working or striving to meet needs, we choose to put the Kingdom first. When we focus on trying to meet the need then our ability to work, produce, or put in the hours becomes the source to meet that need. But when we put the Kingdom first, God takes responsibility for resourcing all that He asks us to do.

RAGS TO RICHES

I had the privilege of attending what is now LeTourneau University to get my engineering degree. R. G. LeTourneau, the founder, was one of the premiere industrialists in his day. But it didn't start that way. After he married his wife Evelyn, life proved tough for the young couple and often they did without necessities. For years they did not even have running water. The death of their first child forced them to realize they had neglected God in their marriage. They committed themselves fully to the Lord and began to tithe. He considered going into ministry, but a pastor friend told him that God needed businessmen too, so he decided to become a businessman for God.

During this time he took a side job of leveling a farmer's field. His frustrations with moving dirt drove him to find a better, more efficient way. In 1922 he constructed the first all-welded scraper that was lighter, stronger and less expensive than any other machines in existence. The year of the stock market crash he formed his earth-moving business. Despite the great depression, LeTourneau succeeded and became one of the greatest obstacle-movers in history. So successful, in fact, that during World War II he produced 70% of all the army's earth-moving machinery. He always attributed his success to the decision he made to make God the Chairman of the Board.

He was hugely successful, with nearly 300 inventions, and filing for hundreds of patents in his lifetime. As he succeeded financially, he increased his giving to the point where he was giving 90% of his income to the Lord's work.[11] LeTourneau said that the money came in faster than he could give it away. He once said, "I shovel out the money, and God shovels it back - but God has a bigger shovel." He was convinced that he could not out-give God.

As a multi-millionaire, LeTourneau continued to live on only 10% of His income. No surprise that his life verse was *seek ye first the kingdom of God and His righteousness and all these things shall be added unto you* (Matt 6:33). Now we may be thinking, "I could give 90% too if I was a multi-millionaire." Maybe so, but the challenge for us is that whatever percentage we currently give, we decide to bump it up with every opportunity.

ABUNDANCE TO GIVE

Looking through the New Testament promises that speak of abundance, most of them are directly tied to us having an abundance to give away. We should expect to have a more than sufficient supply for everything we need, and even some of our wants. But if we miss the fact that the promise of abundance is tied to what we give, the supply God desires to give through us will be limited. If we want to live in abundance, then we must believe to give in abundance. This is a core principle on the road to walking into the abundance that God has for us. Look at how Paul says it: *and God is able to make all grace abound to you, so that always having all sufficiency in everything, you may have an abundance for every good deed* (2 Cor 9:8).

One purpose of God's grace at work in us is that we would have all sufficiency for everything that we need; but also, that we'd have an abundance to give. We still struggle with the concept of "give to get" but we do not have any problem at all with the idea of "give to give." It removes any selfish motive and sets our priorities on the advancement of the Kingdom of God. We don't believe it is difficult for God to get resources to us; the question is can He release His resources through us? Can He trust us to give extravagantly when He blesses us extravagantly? If we would live with an understanding that the purpose of abundance is to give, it would change the way we do business and add generosity into our life and into our call.

The grace of God works in us to release abundance. But the step into abundance comes when we accept His grace to give it away. Look back at the context of the promise of abundance and we see that it is tied directly to giving.

> *Now this I say, he who sows sparingly will also reap sparingly, and he who sows bountifully will also reap bountifully. Each one must do just as he has purposed in his heart, not grudgingly or under compulsion, for God loves a cheerful giver* (2 Cor 9:6, 7).

We see several key attitudes in this passage. The first ties abundance to an attitude of willingness. Are we willing for Him to make us ones who live in abundance? Some Christians are afraid of money. We often refer to money as the "root of all evil." No, it's not; that's a misquote. **The love of money** is the root of evil; the love of money will have us hang on to it instead of giving it away. Money itself is not evil; money is simply a mechanism for expanding the Kingdom. Are we willing for God to release abundance into us so that we can release it into others? Or, will we live with a self-centered mindset that holds the blessing to ourselves?

Paul says we're to give as we purpose in our heart, meaning that our giving reveals our heart attitude. Because giving flows from the heart, we shouldn't give grudgingly or under compulsion. Rather, we are to hear the Spirit of God and respond to His voice. This moves us beyond the attitude of willingness and explains why we sow and reap. The question here is this: Are we giving for ourselves or for others? Do we hold on to the sowing and reaping promise with selfish motives or do we sow with the intention of having an abundance to give? It is true that if we give sparingly we will reap sparingly, and if we give abundantly or generously we're going to reap abundance. But the "why" is important.

Paul makes a direct connection between our giving into the Kingdom of God and our access to walking in abundance. These are not two separate issues. We believe the time has come to step into greater abundance than we've ever known. Somebody once said, "God can always get it to you if He can get it through you." We believe God is going to get more to us than we've ever imagined so He can get it through us into His work.

The third attitude that releases abundance is joy. God loves a cheerful giver. Joy is such a central kingdom value that it serves as an excellent indicator of our heart attitude. If we give with joy, we are operating out of abundance. We've seen an attitude of willingness, an attitude of unselfish sowing and reaping, and an attitude of joy. Give with willingness, with joy and without a selfish motive and we are promised sufficiency for us and an abundance to give away.

PROPORTIONAL AND EXTRAVAGANT

Paul also spoke to the capacity of our giving. He testified that … *according to their ability, and beyond their ability, they gave of their own accord* (2 Cor 8:3). Notice again the reference to willingness; they gave of their own accord, with no manipulation or coercion. People need to give willingly; we will never get to abundance by giving unwilling or grudgingly. Then we read that they gave according to their ability, that's proportional giving. There is a part of our giving that needs to be proportional to our means or income. But then it also says that they gave beyond their ability. This refers to an extravagant kind of giving that's more than proportional. We believe God wants to teach us the breadth of what He's capable of releasing in and through us as we learn to give His way.

We see at least five kinds of giving in the scripture and we could probably list more. Although some of these come from patterns found under the law, the principles behind them still apply as responses to the grace we have received. First, there is the tithe; a proportional kind of giving that is motivated by obedience. It refers to a proportion of our income that we choose to give willingly and joyfully to God's work; we could call it Giving 101. The second kind of giving is first fruits, also a proportional giving, but this time motivated out of expectancy and generosity. We give first fruits when we are looking for an increase, and in anticipation, we give a portion of what we believe God is about to release.

The third is almsgiving, a response giving motivated by compassion. Seeing a need and responding out of compassion to meet it is a legitimate way to give. God gives special promises to us when we meet the needs of the poor. The fourth category of giving is sowing and reaping, a strategic kind of giving motivated by faith. We sow with the expectation of a harvest so that we have an abundance to invest into the Kingdom. The fifth kind of giving is the gift of giving.

THE GIFT OF GIVING

The gift of giving is extravagant giving, motivated by the Holy Spirit. This is a Spirit-driven and Spirit-directed kind of giving.

And Paul tells us that over-the-top abundance is one of the main characteristics. *Since we have gifts that differ according to the grace given to us, each of us is to exercise them accordingly…. he who gives, with liberality…* (Rom 12:6,8). The nature of this gift is *liberality*; the Greek word used here means *sincerely, generously, without pretense or hypocrisy.* It even carries the idea that the gift could be given in secret, demonstrating that there are no strings attached or hidden motives in exercising their gift.

We believe that God will raise up many people with a gift of giving in this next season. Those who step into the gift of giving as their calling will embrace a new mindset that God wants to create in us. They will be excellent stewards who deliberately adjust their lifestyles in order to give more. They will build their lives around the idea of extravagant giving; knowing they have a spiritual gift that extends the reach of the kingdom. Their fruit doesn't just spread the gospel now, but what they give has eternal value because they have vested themselves to see the Kingdom advance.

We believe God wants to change how we see finance and how we understand its value. So bring on the givers with the faith to give greater percentages of their income. No strings attached givers who don't give based on what they have left over; they choose to give 30%, 50% or even an outrageous 90% of their income, making sacrifices with the intention of always giving more.

The purpose of the gift of giving is to encourage and provide for the advancement of the Kingdom of God. As such, it is just as important as any other gift of the Spirit. The gift of giving flows out of hearts of gratefulness at God's love and provision. They give joyfully as an overflow of thanksgiving. The gift of giving is generous; givers love to share the abundant love and grace that God has given them. The gift stays expectant; they are always looking for ways and opportunities to help. The gift is also compassionate, when someone shares a need they rejoice to meet it.

Some of us are waiting until we get our first million before we become generous. But we would suggest that it doesn't work that way. If we haven't been generous with the first dollar, we won't be generous with the millionth dollar. There will always be some reason why we don't yet have enough to give away. Paul explained this when he wrote, *For if the readiness is present, it is acceptable according to what a person has, not according to what he does not have* (2 Cor 8:12). There is an important principle here. We will never become an abundant giver if we don't start now. Become an abundant giver based on what we have available. God looks for a heart attitude of readiness, which looks for opportunities to give.

God is challenging us as His people, to ask Him how to become generous in this next season, generous with giving our time, our resources, our energy, and our finance. We need to ask ourselves, "How can I become a generous person?" How can I begin to live with a selfless generosity that releases His abundance? Because when we surrender to the call of God there is abundance available to us. We may not understand what that looks like, but we have got to believe for more than we've yet experienced. We have got to learn to give motivated by the Spirit. We have got to learn to give beginning with what we have in our hand right now, so that as God increases His favor in our finance, time, energy, resources, we automatically give more.

When we get that nice crisp $100 bill in a Christmas card, is our first instinct to think about what we are going to buy? Or is our first instinct to ask, "Who is this for?" If we ask who it is for, then our instinct came from abundance. When we ask, God may say spend it, but at least ask the question first. If we don't start asking abundance questions, we're never going to get to abundance, because abundance is released from a fundamental generosity in the people of God. It is a generous response to His love for us.

Sometimes we want the law to release grace but the reality is that tithing based on the law is at best a starting minimum for what God wants to do in us. We do believe in tithing, it is the first check we write every week. That's a habit of life for us. We give the tithe before we start giving and then, having given, we give as much as it's possible at every opportunity. Why? Because we choose to believe for even more abundance than we've walked in, way more than we've understood. Paul promised us that *He who supplies seed to the sower and bread for food will supply and multiply your seed for sowing and increase the harvest of your righteousness* (2 Cor 9:10). When we learn to give motivated by the Spirit, He will multiply the seed needed to sow for an abundant harvest.

If we don't have seed to sow, ask Him for seed. The next time twenty bucks shows up in our birthday card, think about who it's for before we think about us. How would you give if you knew He was bringing you great abundance? There's a financial stewardship that we need to step into and walk into in this next season. We think God will train us in some principles over the next couple of years, which are the truth we need to fulfill all He asks of us. Get ready for abundance.

The Call of God
An Invitation to Team

Steve a new truck salesman writes – When I was twelve, I went to a Revival with my mom in the small town of Bois D'Arc, Missouri. Toward the end of the revival, Pastor Paul asked what I wanted to be when I grew up, and I told him that I wanted to be a diesel mechanic. He brought me up to the front and prayed over me. Today – 25 years later – after working as a diesel mechanic, manager of a repair shop, and now in sales, I can say that the Lord has used me to give faith and vision to others through my job.

I remember when a young mechanic just out of college joined our team. He learned very quickly and made few mistakes; however, when I spoke with the seasoned mechanics, I found out that no one liked him. The next time I met with the young man, I asked him how he felt working in our shop. He struggled to answer, then began to cry. He said "no one likes me and they talk about me behind my back." I could see the pain that he suffered and I started to encourage him and speak into his life. I prayed with him and showed him how the bible tells us to treat others. He responded well and immediately others could see the change. Thanks to Jesus, He frees us and fills us with abundant life.

AN INVITATION TO TEAM

God created us to function in community, not in isolation. The community provides the context where we share life together, where we fellowship with each other, and through these loving relationships grow into maturity. We all need this environment for our own development. But community doesn't stop with fellowship. The same concept extends out into our mission. We are invited to function in our calling and gifting in teams as an extension of our life in community. While the context of community is vital for our growth and development, it proves just as crucial for anyone who carries the kingdom lifestyle out into the world. We were not created to function in isolation. God created us to work, learn, minister, and change the world by finding those who will walk beside us in team. We need each other!

David, the man after God's heart, gives us a glimpse of the kind of leadership and team that God has designed. One thing that made him such a great leader was that he surrounded himself with a team of mighty men. But they didn't start out that way; when they joined David they were anything but leadership material - distressed, in debt and running from the law. However, when we choose to lead with God's heart, those around us will respond and step into their destiny as well. These men did great exploits with David and served him for his entire reign. Three of them grew into leaders of the mighty men, showing us that David was secure enough to delegate and grow leaders.

COME AND SEE

Jesus demonstrated the same model when He called His disciples to be with Him. Their primary training would take place in the interaction they shared in community. They would not be formally trained; they were discipled by the fellowship with Him and their interactions with each other. Jesus invited Andrew, one of John's disciples to "come and see;" it was an open invitation to him as well as a promise, that if he would say yes, he would experience the goodness of God through fellowship with a community of believers. It was an invitation to join Jesus' team of disciples to be trained and sent out to fulfill their calling.

We see the same phrase used by Philip who encourages his friend Nathanael to "come and see." He is inviting his friend to come and experience something special that he had found. To fulfill the call of God we are each invited to come and see what it looks like to work in team. To look for and taste a model of leadership and ministry that is different than anything we have experienced before. To come and see what happens when brothers and sisters begin to work together, sharing their strengths and covering each other's weaknesses. To come and see what happens when we choose to use our gifts to compliment one another, not to compete. Come and see what it looks like to work in team.

We started out as the typical "we-can-do-it-all-without-any-help" individualistic missionaries. However, years of pruning and a deep work of the Spirit have slowly changed us to value team ministry. We have learned the importance of a culture of honor and understand the need for a diversity of gifts to work together in compliment. And we have, more specifically, come to realize our desperate need for others. The life-lessons that have brought us to this place are numerous and painful, but they have birthed a hunger in us to see the true unity of the body demonstrated in and through team ministry.

This pruning work of the Spirit has taken a variety of shapes, but perhaps the most telling has come through our role of caring for pastors and leaders. Over the years we have watched as some who we would call friends have fallen victim to the isolation of ministry. Several times we have served as part of the team to counsel and help restore them to ministry. In the process, we have found a common theme. Most of them, when we got down to the root cause, acknowledged that they had allowed themselves to get isolated, sometimes even from their spouse. And in the place of isolation fell victim to temptation.

Why do we do this? Why do great and gifted ministries too often seem to self-destruct? There must be something we are missing. It is easy to blame it on character weakness or lack of accountability, and unquestionably that plays a part, but we believe that the problem is much more fundamental. There is a flaw in the foundation of our understanding of our place and position as leaders and a misunderstanding of our need for real relationship with others that sets us up for this kind of failure. If we do not see ourselves as God sees us and allow the revelation to radically alter the way we walk with others, there is no answer but to clean up the broken pieces.

THE MISSING LINK

In the creation of man, God said that it was not good for man to be alone. We can see several reasons for this; clearly it did not express the plurality of the Godhead and the need for procreation. But another important reason is that He created us for fellowship, with a need for social interaction with others. God designed us with the capacity and the need to form deep and lasting relationships. We function at our best when these life-giving relationships are in place and at our most vulnerable when we feel alone.

The temptation of Jesus took place in isolation in the desert. Scripture tells us that Jesus was tempted in the same ways we are tempted, so it stands to reason that His temptation took place in solitude, demonstrating that isolation is the place of greatest vulnerability. When we stand together we can take on most any adversary, but get us alone and our insecurities make us easier targets for the schemes of the tempter. When Israel as a nation made their exit from Egypt one of the most important instructions they were given was to stay together. If they did not, they became easy targets for their enemies.

Isolation means to be in a place or situation separate from others. The word originated in the Latin word *insulatus*, which means *made into an island*. When we isolate ourselves, we become an island unto ourselves. For some this may seem like paradise, after all, we like our privacy and all benefit from times of solitude. However, the danger with isolation is not occasional alone time. The difficulties begin to appear when isolation becomes a lifestyle. We were not designed for seclusion; God's call is to build teams in preparation for the harvest.

MENDING THE NET

God's answer for mending the net and weaving a network strong enough to contain the end time harvest is a revelation of real committed relationships. Working in team provides the encouragement and accountability we all need to keep us focused on our mission. These relationships cover our weaknesses and help identify and release us into our strengths. Even at its best, the accountability of team is only as good as a person's willingness to stay open. So, for it to work we each need to embrace an internal work of the Spirit that causes us to want to remain vulnerable to others.

We have found ourselves alone more times than we want to count, but slowly we have learned the value of true friends in ministry. This grows in us as we learn that to work together in the body of Christ, we must begin to understand the implications of the New Covenant on our relationships. Too often we have treated lightly our commitment to one another, resulting in a divided and ineffective church. If we will learn to walk together and stay together, then the headship of Christ is established and the growth of the body becomes natural. We each need to ask the Holy Spirit to give us a revelation of our need for each other. Let Him show us how relationships can provide the key to effective ministry. Ask Him to help us understand that at our very best and most anointed, we are still incomplete by design.

INCOMPLETE BY DESIGN

Remember, before the creation of Eve, Adam was alone and his isolation was the only thing in all creation that God referred to as "not good." His answer to this deficiency was to put Adam into team. The process of creating Eve as a helpmate for Adam was both fascinating and intricate. God takes something out of Adam, permanently disabling him. Never again would he, or anyone alone, be able to perfectly represent his or her Creator. That would now be done only as a team. Only together would they represent the image of the plurality of the Godhead. To read more of the scriptural foundation for this, the first few chapters of our book, *Incomplete by Design*, goes into much more detail and lays a broader scriptural foundation.

A leader in isolation represents a broken model of church leadership. It is distressing that we have taken the one thing God said was not good and made it the primary model for bringing His body to spiritual maturity. No wonder we struggle to accomplish this task.

We are neglecting other parts of the body that carry different gifts and anointings, which are necessary to bring believers into their destiny as His priests and ministers. Spiritual maturity or completeness can never be found in isolation. Maturity is a process that demands interaction with other believers, meaning that we can't come to maturity without community.

God does not see us separate but as parts of the whole. Under the New Covenant, He sees us as single parts that together form His glorious body, the Church. We need this revelation! We are parts coming together to make up a whole, His body, His Church. Paul tells the church that the Father put all things under the feet of His Son (Eph1:23). Christ, our head, fulfilled His ministry as the perfect and complete apostle, prophet, evangelist, pastor and teacher (Eph 4:12). But when He returned to His Father after His resurrection He released these facets of His ministry into the earth to work in us.

His ministry continues through us with these same distinct facets that we refer to now as the fivefold ministry. Christ, the perfect and complete representation of the gifts, has so designed the body that no single individual carries all five of these ministries. We each have a unique part, but our part functions best as a part of the whole. We are individually incomplete by design and we can only represent the whole of who Jesus is when we work together. This means that it is fundamentally impossible to ever bring the body of Christ to maturity without team ministry in some form!

JESUS' MODEL

Jesus built His life and ministry around relationships. As a child, he took opportunity to sit at the feet of teachers and learn from those who had studied and gone before. One of the remarkable parts of that story was that it took three days before his parents missed him. That means that he spent a bunch of time with his friends, in fact so much that being with and relating to other families was normal life. When He performed His first miracle, Mary His own mother was the team member that activated the moment.

When He called His disciples He invited them to be with Him. They ate together, slept together, laughed together, and ministered together. They literally shared their lives with one another. Scripture gives us a glimpse into a wide variety and depth of relationships in the ministry life of Jesus. He called the twelve to be with Him as close working companions but even within the twelve, Peter, James and John were occasionally off with Jesus alone. They seemed to have a closer relationship than the others. Then there is John, who developed a relationship of even greater depth.

The Call of God
An Invitation to Family

Ralph, owner of a printing business writes – The connection of the secular and spiritual in the marketplace within my influence has required a paradigm shift in how I approach different situations. The question I ask myself is, "What would the Father have me do?" The answer I receive frames my response to the experiences that present themselves. It could mean just listening and speaking a word of encouragement that directs people to recognize how good God is, or stopping and praying for a physical or mental hurt. It's an adventure, which requires a courage that only God can give through His Spirit dwelling in me. I have had the opportunity to forgive mountains of debt owed to me and see how it affected the person and drew them closer to God. That was a price I am glad I paid.

The greatest compliment someone can give me is when he or she recognizes that I didn't respond like they expected. This provides a great opportunity to direct them to the strength and wisdom that God gives. One of the most challenging moments of my business life was the decision to refuse to declare bankruptcy because of the harm it would bring to all my creditors, vendors and lenders. It would have been easy to get rid of a huge financial problem, but would not have been the right decision. The experiences of living the Kingdom out in my everyday work life are numerous and I am glad for the opportunity to live them.

Team Relationships

Within any team, there will be and should be a variety of relationships much like in a natural family. In the family, some relationships give life, while others are only distant acquaintances. But the relationships that shape us the most are those in the immediate family. These break down into three definable relationship dynamics; the parents, our siblings and the children. We will examine these three relational spheres in a team context as first, Models and Mentors, second Partners and Friends, and finally Sons and Daughters. Of course, the family is much more complicated than this and we left out the most fun, which is the grandchildren. But as we will see, ministry teams should reflect some form of these relational dynamics.

Models and Mentors

Our relationships within a team will take on several forms, but one of the most crucial is to find models or mentors. If we want to be fully equipped, we need to find advisors in each season of our life who will model the aspect of life and ministry we are seeking to pursue. We must seek out those willing to invest in us as mentors to help us grow and nurture our gifts. We all need models that inspire us. Jesus said *I gave you an example that you also should do as I did to you* (Jn 13:15). He set the pattern through His life and ministry and encourages us to do the same. Which leads to the question: Who are we following? Who are the models in our life? It is easy to say Jesus and it even sounds spiritual, but the nature of team ministry requires us to find those relationships, which represent Jesus well and follow their example.

Sally and I have had several people who fit into this category of relationship. We have had mentors who poured into our prayer life while others helped us come out of legalism. The most strategic for us was when the Lord brought Philip Mohabir into our lives. He was a seasoned apostolic father who had planted scores of churches and knew how to train leaders. As our relationship grew, Phil became the spiritual father I needed and we invited him to speak into our lives. He never assumed rights that we did not give him and never asked for more than we offered, but soon we found ourselves hungry for all we knew he had to give.

This led to a relationship of mentoring where he asked questions about every area of our life, marriage, and ministry. With Phil, we got down to the real issues of how we managed our time and relationships. He set a pattern for our spiritual development and left nothing out. The long walks with him were both pleasant and painful as he asked difficult questions.

We will never forget traveling to London to visit him. He would always answer the door with a question; looking at Sally's face he would ask me how we were doing. By the expression on her face he would instantly know the truth and for the next few hours, he would share life with us. We look back at this period as a precious gift because it changed us forever, molding our marriage, our relationships with others and released us into effective ministry.

We didn't always take his advice but most of the time when we didn't we later wished that we had. We drew from his wisdom and experience and found ourselves emulating his characteristics and responses. We truly received a mantle of apostolic authority and insight. We learned from him the process of restoring a fallen brother and learned how to exercise grace and mercy without compromise. It might be slightly idealized with time but to us he walked a perfect blend of humility and authority.

This need for models and mentors was confirmed by Paul when he encouraged us, to *join in following my example, and observe those who walk according to the pattern you have in us* (Phil 3:17). We need mentors to advise us and give us their wisdom and counsel. We see this in scripture in the relationship between Elisha and Elijah, which ends up releasing the double portion blessing.

So what qualifies a person to function as a spiritual father or mother? Solomon tells us that *good advice lies deep within a counselor's heart, the wise man will draw it out* (Pro 20:5). To receive from someone they must have something spiritually that we want or need and be willing to share it with us. They will demonstrate the character and nature of Christ in such a way that they are worth following. We benefit from a mentor by first pursuing them and then asking questions to draw out the wisdom we need.

True spiritual fathers and mothers will challenge us to shape our character. The great value of a mentor is that they see the things we are blind to and help shape us into the image of Christ by walking with us in a relationship of trust and loyalty. Although spiritual fathers and mothers are willing to walk in long-term accountability, as a rule they don't pursue us. We must decide to pursue them and draw from them all we need. We first thought this was somehow unfair, but today as spiritual parents we realize that anyone we have to chase is not really looking for change; they are only looking for our affirmation.

Partners and Friends

Partners and friends form the second category of relationships within a team. Scripture tells us that,

> ...*two can accomplish more than twice as much as one, for the results can be much better. If one falls, the other pulls him up; but if a man falls when he is alone, he's in trouble* (Ecc 4:9, 10).

God's design for us is to work in team with others so that together we can be more effective in fulfilling our individual and corporate functions. When we are together we achieve more than we ever would alone. The peer relationships in team provide strength by exercising their gifts to fill out areas where we lack. The different gifts working together present a more complete representation of the fullness of Christ.

The partnership we experience in team ministry is more than just functional; team members become friends that support us. True friends give us a secure foundation to step out and take a risk. Solomon in his wisdom said that *a friend loves at all times, and a brother is born for adversity* (Pro 17:17). Friendship within a team means there are people who really know us and with whom we can share our hearts. They know our strengths and weaknesses and still accept us. When there is a true bond of mutual affection with a friend, we get the support and encouragement we need to fulfill our call.

When we think of being in partnership with others, we understand that the bond of the relationship provides the key to working together. We see this in operation in the church when Paul writes, *so we, who are many, are one body in Christ, and individually members one of another* (Rom 12:4, 5). The implications of the New Covenant on our relationships mean that we learn to stay together even through the difficult times. The imagery for this in scripture is the supply that flows through the joints in the body and the relational power of the ligaments that keep us together (Col 2:19). Through the challenges of working together, we learn to not just accept one another, we learn to receive from one another.

Just as Jethro came to Moses and instructed him, team members can bring us the wisdom we need to hear. Moses was the leader, he had the word of the Lord and the anointing to lead, but God sent a father-in-law to give His leader needed instruction. It is true that *he who walks with wise men will be wise, but the companion of fools will suffer harm* (Pro 13:20). I will never forget the first time Randy, one of the elders in our team here in Springfield, came in his quiet, gentle way and brought me a correction. At first, I almost didn't know how to take it, but then realized that God had given me exactly what I needed, a partner and friend who would be honest.

The idea of partnership does away with the feeling of being over or under each other and allows us to walk as peers. While we recognize that most teams in scripture did have a leader, we suggest that the leadership needed for team ministry to function fully is more of a "first among equals" than a one-man show. This allows the members of a team the freedom to share what they are hearing and feeling in a safe atmosphere.

When we accept that others have a part of what we need, it changes the nature of our relationships. We genuinely begin to want the best for each other and as the writer of Hebrews says, we *consider how we may spur one another on toward love and good deeds* (Heb. 10:24). When we operate this way we find real support, a foundation we need to complete all God has given us to do. God did not design us to do it on our own; He created us to fulfill His purpose in vital union with Him and with one another. We need both to succeed.

SONS AND DAUGHTERS

Pouring ourselves into the next generation should be one of our highest priorities. The last verse in the Old Testament shows that paternity is still God's intention. The prophet Malachi promises that the Lord will *restore the hearts of the fathers to their children, and the hearts of the children to their fathers* (Mal 4:6). This prophetic promise will have a fulfillment. The last days will bring a restoration of the spirit of Elijah, a prophetic spirit that compels fathers and mothers to emerge and turn toward their children. It will at the same time cause children to realign themselves with their natural and spiritual parents.

The Church today is in desperate need of fathers and mothers who know God and are willing to take responsibility to bring the next generation into leadership alongside them. Paul, as the spiritual father to Timothy, urges the Corinthians to follow his example (1 Cor 4:16). True mentors are bold enough to set an example, yet humble enough to pour themselves into the lives of others.

This will require leaders to focus on the development and training of the next generation, rather than concentrating on their own purpose and ministry. John McElroy admits, "Like many of my contemporaries in ministry, I became caught up in the race to ascend the ladder. Sadly, I had become more enamored with innovative leadership programs and getting things done than on spending quality time building into spiritual sons and daughters."[12] Malachi's word

135

indicates that the fathers and mothers must act first. Their hearts must turn toward their sons and daughters so that they are prepared to receive them, love them and invest their lives into them.

Effective team ministry should reflect some form of all three of these relationship dynamics if we hope to fulfill our purpose. We must pursue spiritual fathers and mothers who can sharpen us and impart wisdom we need to fulfill our calling. We need partners and friends who walk beside us, free to exercise their gifts as they carry responsibility with us. We also need a deliberate focus to pass on what we have learned as a legacy because we were born to make our ceiling the ground floor for the next generation

The Call of God
An Invitation to Legacy

Danika, a bank vice president, writes: Recently I have been reflecting on how much favor I have had in a major bank. Anyone that works at my level in this industry must have a degree and preferably a master's degree. I don't have either; yet the Lord continues to give me favor, not only with promotions over the years but favor with senior leadership everywhere I go. Anyone that works alongside of me knows my relationship with Jesus, but I don't push it on them; I just live my life focused on pleasing Christ and allow others to see Him working in and through me. As a result, it is common for people I work with to ask me to pray for family or other situations they are facing.

I have often asked the Lord why He has me here. What's my purpose? It has to be bigger than this. After thirteen years and with knowing my plans of hopefully retiring soon, I now report directly to a gentleman here on a two-year visa that just happens to be a self-proclaimed atheist. I don't know what it will look like or how, but the Lord has given me so much favor with this new boss and I am trusting that before we go our separate ways, God is going to get the glory. Whether that's leading him directly to Christ or planting seeds. Either way I will allow the Lord to use me however He can to save just one!

137

AN INVITATION TO LEGACY

Our English word legacy comes from a Latin word meaning commission. When we respond to the call of God, He commissions us to represent Him. Our duties require us to live in, demonstrate and extend His kingdom here on earth. To do this effectively we must understand heaven's value system, which opens our minds to God's eternal perspective. The call of God has eternal consequences, meaning first that we will each give an account of our stewardship of the call. But as well, the extent to which we fulfill our commission ultimately defines the legacy we leave for the next generation.

Once we know God has called us, something must change in us so that we begin to put value on the things He values. As human beings we tend to focus on the temporal, meaning that we direct our energies and effort into the natural realm we can see and touch. The chair we sit on feels more real than the spiritual realm around us. But in truth, the spiritual realm is just as real, if not more real, because it is eternal. God created us to interact and participate with Him in the unseen eternal realm. When we surrender to the call, the Holy Spirit teaches us to live with an eternal perspective that adjusts our focus so we can live in God's economy. This renewal of our mind is crucial to accomplishing all God has called us to do.

When we understand that our calling has eternal implications, it will adjust our behaviors by changing some ways we think and respond. We need God to help us see what we do not see, so we can we learn to leave an eternal inheritance. In the rest of this chapter, we will suggest three priorities for building a spiritual legacy. Each represents a key mind shift that will help us move out of a temporal perspective. We never get beyond the need to challenge our thinking, to check our hearts and to measure our actions against God's kingdom standards.

SEEK FIRST THE KINGDOM

We can't live the true nature of our call without embracing our kingdom identity as a first priority. We can talk about it, think about it, discuss it and even come up with some good ideas. But putting the kingdom first means that we look at life through a different pair of eyes. We begin to see the difference between things that are temporal and those things or activities that have real eternal consequence. Prioritizing the kingdom has a real and direct effect on the future of our life and the lives of the next generation. The more eternal we become in the way we think and act, the more we will truly represent the Kingdom of God here on earth.

God has placed in each of us a hunger and a drive to build something that lasts. Everyone wants to leave something, make something, or even put our name on something. We all want to leave a legacy. Jesus tells us that the key to the fulfillment of our purpose in life is to *seek first His kingdom and His righteousness, and all these things will be added to you* (Matt 6:33). He asks those who respond to His call to focus on living in and extending the Kingdom of God as their first concern. He promises that when we get our priorities right, we will not only accomplish our call, but we will have access to the resources necessary to fulfill it and create a sustaining legacy.

To seek first the kingdom means we focus on building His kingdom rather than building something for ourself. We find that we have to regularly check our motivation for ministry. Sally and I want to leave a legacy, but the legacy we leave isn't a structure. It isn't about the material realm, what we've put in bricks and mortar. The legacy we want to leave is a thought system, a kingdom culture, and a way of behaving that will affect the next generation. That's the real legacy. We all want something to define and outlast us, but God looks for people willing to give their lives to build His kingdom and let that stand as our legacy.

To seek first the kingdom we must understand the relationship between the Kingdom of God and the work of the Holy Spirit. Being full of the Spirit must be more than a Christian catchphrase. We can't build the Kingdom of God with self-effort; the Lord told Zerubbabel that it was *not by might or by power, but by His Spirit* (Zech 4:6). The measure of whether we're succeeding must be the presence of the Holy Spirit evidenced in our lives. God invites us to live in vital relationship with the Holy Spirit. When we give ourselves to being possessed by the Holy Spirit, we become a people of His presence. From this place of fellowship and surrender, it becomes easy to live with an eternal supernatural kingdom perspective.

The Kingdom of God is expressed through our walk in the Holy Spirit, which means that people who seek first the kingdom stay hungry to live full of the Spirit. They are people who deliberately make room for the gifts and fruit of the Holy Spirit to work through them. Scripture promises us that if we get this relationship right we release a multigenerational blessing. David wrote,

> *how blessed is the man who fears the Lord, who greatly delights in His commandments. His descendants will be mighty on the earth. The generation of the upright will be blessed* (Ps 112:1-2).

Remember, David was writing about a law on tablets of stone and we can apply this to the law of the Spirit of life in Christ. So, delighting in obedience to the Holy Spirit has eternal consequence. Giving our lives to building the Kingdom of God will prepare the way for our descendants to be mighty, meaning they get to walk in even more that we have experienced.

If we seek to live full of the Spirit then the next generation gets to live in the blessing, not just of what we've done, but also in the supernatural culture we have prepared. We build an attitude and atmosphere where the Holy Spirit has become so welcome that it is normal for people to walk full of the Holy Spirit. We didn't grow up with that expectation and have had to shift cultures several times through the years to embrace what God is doing in this day. We don't want to miss a moment of this season so we choose to live full of the Spirit. Relationship with the Spirit changes the way we think about life so that our first priority becomes the extension of His kingdom in the earth.

Seeking first the kingdom means learning how to sustain a kingdom culture in our lifestyle so we become an influence for change in the culture around us. In the last few years, business has coined the term "strategic leadership." They define strategic leadership as a leader that can look into the future and prepare a company for things that they don't yet see coming. It sounds very prophetic to us: We need to look into and prepare for where we're going without having to see the full picture in advance. We must live as those who see the unseen (2 Cor 4:18). Quite simply that means surrender to the Holy Spirit and living to extend the Kingdom of God.

Value People Over Ministry

The second principle important to living and leading with an eternal perspective is to invest in people, not in ministry. We must live with a high value for the people God has put in our lives and protect our relationships with them. Many desire to step into a ministry of some kind but we often find they are reluctant to truly invest in people. People are not the means to ministry; they are the ministry. John Maxwell said it this way,

> *Too often, leaders put their energy into organizations, buildings, systems or other lifeless objects, but only people live on after we are gone. Everything else is temporary.*[13]

No ministry we build has any significance unless it focuses on the people God brings to us. If we aren't willing to start with one person, we won't build anything of real value. Only when we invest in people is the Kingdom of God truly advanced. Nothing else in the temporal realm has eternal significance. It is easy to let ministry become the idol we work for instead of being willing to take care of one person, then two, then three, and then ten. It is the lives we touch that matter to God. Just invest in people and let Him work out the value of our investment.

We can look successful in the world's eyes by accumulation of material possessions but only the lives we invest in carry value into the next generation. Our primary energy must go into people, not into systems. Paul told Timothy, his spiritual son that *the things that you have heard from me in the presence of many witnesses, entrust these to faithful men who will be able to teach others also* (2 Tim 2:2). Paul instructs us to entrust the things we learn to people who would pour into people, because it is only when we invest in lives that what we do has eternal value. If we grasp this, it would change the way we live. We are to pour our lives into faithful men and women willing to pass God's truth on to others, then we will have a lasting impact on the next generation.

Instead of looking for a ministry platform, frustrated that we aren't given an opportunity to minister, start with one person. We all have a neighbor, a friend or an acquaintance who needs someone to befriend them, encourage them, and pour into them. Begin to invest into that individual and in doing so we embrace real kingdom value. The Kingdom of God is about people, not platforms; it is about people and not buildings, about people not institutions; it is about people not educational systems. Everything revolves around people and everything must come back to people. If we want a ministry, just love people, care for people, and pour our life into people.

Most successful ministries we relate to started without fanfare. Some took orphans into their home; others worked with the destitute and out of their sacrificial love have grown substantial ministries. But they didn't do it to grow a ministry; they did it to love people. In the act of loving people a ministry grew, but if we ever lose the focus on people then we have lost the heart of everything we do. Every time we invest in an individual we extend the influence of God's kingdom. Through our relationships, His unconditional love spreads to others. Relationships need to have a higher priority to us than any kind of infrastructure. People matter.

David was a man after God's own heart. His love for God led to a desire to build God's house, but God said he could not do it. Instead, David invested in his son who would fulfill the dream of his heart. Heaven sees things differently than we do; the Kingdom of God thinks multi-generationally. Heaven does not look at our generation and see an end or limit based on our lifespan. God's eternal perspective sees a seamless flow of Kingdom life into the earth from generation to generation.

Heaven's perspective sees continuity from one generation to another. He is the God of Abraham, Isaac and Jacob. If we are going to create a true kingdom culture, we must begin to think like heaven so that the things we build or create have value to the next generation. We want them to enjoy and share in a culture where people love each other, a culture where people honor each other, a culture where people put people first and a culture where relationships matter. As we labor to bring heaven to earth we must do it consistent with heaven's value system, a system based on the price the Father was willing to pay for one individual, the blood of His Son.

I remember as a teenager when my value system got rocked. Perhaps because I grew up on the mission field, I enjoyed reading missionary stories. As I read the story of Amy Carmichael and her work in India, I ran across a dream she recorded. It was a lengthy dream about huge crowds of people walking blindly off a cliff, and her efforts to warn them. She wrote,

> *...once a girl stood alone in her place, waving the people back; but her mother and other relations called and reminded her that her furlough was due; she must not break the rules. And being tired and needing a change, she had to go and rest for awhile; but no one was sent to guard her gap, and over and over the people fell, like a waterfall of souls.*[14]

The phrase "waterfall of souls" wrecked me. The image was so graphic that the words still live in my mind. God's perspective is His love for people. His call on our lives, no matter our profession, is to labor to stem the tide of souls falling to destruction. The call of God must focus on people because only people have eternal value to Him. He paid for them with the precious blood of His own Son.

God, help us to adjust our value system to line up with Yours.

Ownership or Influence

The third foundation for living with an eternal perspective requires that we learn to live for influence, not for ownership. In the early days of the apostolic ministry being restored, church leaders tended to use a lot of ownership language. They had clear divisions between "my" churches and "your" churches. One apostolic leader told us that the city we had moved to was his city and if we were going to work there, we needed to submit to him. There was a lot of ownership mentality in the way things were done. When we adopt an ownership mindset we limit the scope of what God can do in and through us.

While we see ownership as a problem in some of the teachings we have heard about the kingdom, there is a legitimate use of the word ownership. We believe people need to own the vision of where we're going. We need to own the responsibility God gives us. So there is a correct use of the word ownership. But there is also a kind of ownership in the Church that is out of balance. Perhaps we should have used the word "control" instead of ownership but we want to go to the root of a misuse and the word God spoke to us was that He wants us to live for influence, not for ownership.

STEWARDS OF GRACE

The challenge with the idea of ownership is that scripture clearly teaches that the Church belongs to Jesus. It is His! Webster defines ownership as the state of being an owner, legal right of possession, or proprietorship. Jesus clearly is the proprietor while we serve simply as stewards of all that He has entrusted to us. Peter introduces this word when he wrote, *each one has received a special gift, employ it in serving one another as good stewards of the manifold grace of God* (1 Pet 4:10). When we live as stewards it changes the nature of our assignment.

The word *steward* means manager, overseer, an employee, a treasurer or even a preacher. When we lead as stewards we understand that the responsibility we carry is for others, not for ourselves. The calling we have received came to us by grace, not our works. We now must learn to be good stewards and stop trying to own His stuff. Someone once said that owners can kill and eat the sheep but stewards give themselves to only protect the flock. So often we want to own that which does not belong to us.

LIVING TO INFLUENCE

Influence is defined in the dictionary as the capacity or power of a person to be a compelling force or to produce effects on the action, behavior, and opinion of others. It can also mean the action or process of producing effects, actions, and behavior on others. When we go for influence we get to affect what other people think. We get to affect the actions of other people but we do it without having any ownership over them. When we've sold out to influence rather than to ownership it gets rid of many barriers, borders, and limitations.

Teams can start working with each other and get the best of what each other has, because we are not in competition; we're living for influence. We're not trying to own what somebody else is doing. We really believe that God wants to kill this ownership tendency in the body of Christ.

Instead, He wants a people who live to influence the actions, behaviors, and opinions in Christian culture. When we live to influence, our investment has eternal consequence because the actions and behaviors of people affect their destiny. By opting for influence rather than ownership we get to influence the next generation with things that are truly eternal. What if we just tried to influence the culture in our city and didn't worry so much about which church they belong to. It sounds scary. Now, we do think people need to know where they belong but some of our concerns are more tied to ownership than to influence.

The word *influence* comes from the Latin word *influere*, a compound word that means *to flow into*. The original idea of the word was a reference to flowing matter. When we live for influence, something flows through us into others. When you choose to live from influence as a leader, Heaven's culture flows through us like matter. Influence literally has substance and flows out to the people that we are touching. Choose to live as a conduit of influence that comes from heaven rather than living to possess something here on earth.

INSECURITY AND OWNERSHIP

We all have insecurities, especially as leaders. The consequence of insecurity causes us to tend toward ownership because it feels more secure. When we own it we can define it, protect it, and our boundaries are clear. But the answer to insecurity is not to hold on tighter, but rather to let go, and allow Jesus to build His church. Matthew tells us there is no need to be anxious about anything. He goes on to say we cannot serve God and mammon. The word mammon is translated as *money* most of the time, but the word comes from an Aramaic root that means self-security. This indicates that we can't serve God and at the same time hold on to things, actions or mindsets that give security to self. We have to choose between living for what gives us security and placing our security in obedience to the call of God.

The implication is that when we serve God it can feel rather insecure unless we fully put our security in Him. That is the nature of the call of God, which brings the question, Are we willing to serve Him and let go of our own insecurity? This is crucial because by definition, insecurity exalts self. When we are insecure we promote ourself in order to feel more secure. Insecurity causes us to hold on to things, to own things and people because it makes us feel better, more successful. So, are we going to live for our own security or are we going to live for influence? When we live for influence, we live with our identity fully in Him and let go of the desperation in us to hold on to what we feel slipping away.

Over the last five years Sally and I have walked through a season in which, as we follow the call, we have come to own less than we have ever owned. We do not currently pastor a church or serve as the primary leader in a ministry. Yet, at the same time we have grown to have more influence than we have ever had in our lives. We believe this is for more than just us; this paradigm shift to living for influence describes how heaven's culture extends. This culture doesn't come by keeping control. It doesn't extend by holding on too tightly to people or things; if we do, we kill it.

No, the kingdom extends as we live for influence with an open hand. It comes as we influence the very next person we meet. It comes as we live to influence their actions, behaviors, and opinions. The kingdom extends as the Holy Spirit moves out through us, releasing the prophetic, a word of knowledge and healing. We influence those we encounter without trying to own them. So, are we looking for ownership or influence? Are we willing to let go of the insecurities that have kept us bound? This will change us!

ATTITUDES OF OWNERSHIP

There are several key transitions that take place in our thinking and motivation. These will not only help us identify subtle attitudes of ownership that lurk in our hearts, but will also help us understand the way forward into greater influence. When we live for ownership we live, work, and minister to make a name for ourself. We need something that has our identity on it. When we live for influence we live to make Jesus famous. We live to change history. We live to change the culture around us and see that new culture passed down from generation to generation. The things that we've learned, fought for, gained, and walked in we can now use to influence other people without having to own them.

Ownership has real boundaries of responsibility. We do believe that God gives us certain people, situations, and churches where He makes us responsible. But even in direct apostolic oversight, when a group or church asks for our regular input, we must not be possessive or try to own them. We want them to be touched by heaven. We want to influence so that life flows from us into them through all we do. As owners, we only have access to that which we own and when we get outside of that sphere we start feeling insecure. On the other hand, when we live for influence we have access to places that we never thought possible and we become an influencer everywhere we go, even outside of our church or network.

Ownership builds for the present, while influence builds for the future. Because of this, ownership focuses on the temporal, things that are here now and that we can clearly define. When we walk in influence, it opens our minds to think like heaven. When we walk in influence, we live with constant future expectation. In that place God gives revelation of how to affect our surroundings. Living to influence changes our perspective at work, at home with our family and at our church. When we live for influence we listen for what God wants to say in this season and we look for what He is doing.

Ownership roots in self-effort, whereas influence flows from the grace of God. When we live from ownership we work to create opportunities and measure success by our achievement. One major problem with this is that we also become subject to burnout. Influence flows from the grace of God. His gift of grace equips us to influence any environment because we live as King's kids. His grace through us touches the lives of individuals we encounter because of the life that flows through us. This is Heaven's culture, living with eternity in mind.

CALLED AS AMBASSADORS

Paul uses the word ambassador as another analogy to describe the nature of our calling and influence. *Therefore, we are ambassadors for Christ, as though God were making an appeal through us; we beg you on behalf of Christ, be reconciled to God* (2 Cor 5:20). The role of an ambassador is to extend the influence of the King into foreign territory. They are sent to represent and influence others on behalf of the Kingdom. The role of an ambassador is not ownership but rather exerting an influence in the new realm by representing and sharing the beliefs and values of the Kingdom of God.

We're called as ambassadors to influence this world for the sake of the King. We believe if we would live for influence, we would get away from the kingdom-building mindset that so easily creeps into leaders of the body of Christ. It infects us even as individuals. We want something that is ours. We want to build something but in the very desperation to do that we lose the influence that God wants to give us.

The word *legacy* appeared in English in the late 14th century with an original meaning of *a body of persons sent on a mission.* It came from the Latin word *legatus* meaning *commission, ambassador, or envoy.* How appropriate that if we are to leave a legacy, we can only do it commissioned as ambassadors or envoys of the King of Kings.

The Call of God
An Invitation Epilogue

Jeff, a professional photographer writes – As a young man I was ordained as a pastor; however, even though I had a soft heart I did not have tough enough skin so I left formal ministry. The Lord led me to start my own photography business. I soon found out that I had more opportunities to share my faith in the marketplace than I ever had as a minister! About six years ago, the Lord told me that I was to now consider myself bi-vocational. It sounded simple enough but it took a year or two for that to really sink in.

Now, I lead a citywide healing prayer ministry and spend more time praying for and training others than I do with my business. I am aware that my "calling" is every bit as intact now as ever. For over 10 years I have been publishing my own coffee table books and my desire is that the people who purchase my books see the hand of the Creator in every image. The Lord continues to bless my business and I am able to bless others in ways that I never imagined. Only Jesus could orchestrate things so that I could be used by Him and that He would receive the glory. Thanks be to God!

EPILOGUE

What an amazing time to be alive. We are living in a season of kingdom expansion in which we are able to release into others the things that we have learned and carried over the years. The body of Christ is beginning to wake up to her responsibility to carry the good news into every corner of society. And at the same time, leadership in this move of God are coming to understand that their responsibility is to equip and release people into ministry rather than to hold on to people out of their need for security.

This is incredibly important. Too often those in church leadership have lived with a possessive mindset, holding on to power, position, or influence. This possessive mindset does not accurately represent Christ's kingdom. His kingdom is actually a very benevolent environment where we are called to constantly give away what we have received in the expectation that there is always more. In giving away what we have received, we develop the capacity for more because there is always more that God has for us.

Several years ago Sally and I were in a large Southern Baptist church in Brazil that had decided they wanted to go for more. They got hungry enough to invite Randy Clark and we watched as they experienced a move of the power and presence of God for the first time. Although much of what they experienced was new, they welcomed the Holy Spirit. You could see some who looked like deer caught in headlights, but despite their hesitation God showed up in a powerful way. Since we have a Baptist history, it was a lot of fun. When we returned the following year to the same church we found they had grown, built a new building and they had fully embraced a life in the Spirit with no loss of momentum.

There is something special in this testimony. As we began to pray after this experience we asked the question, "God, what is it?" What was it in their DNA that so transformed them in such a rapid period of time? What is the foundation? The thing He brought to us was their understanding of the call of God and the Lordship of Christ.

Those touched by the Spirit felt compelled to share what they had experienced with others in response to receiving the good news of the gospel. They understood that it was not just the pastor's responsibility.

When we grasp that divine callings are not limited to church leadership or full-time ministry, it changes the way we each live our lives. A university professor knows he is called to teach because he feels the same anointing of the Holy Spirit in the classroom as an evangelist feels in a crusade. When the call of God begins to have this kind of impact on us things begin to change.

COME YOUR KINGDOM

We are all familiar with the Lord's prayer but some suggest that the language could be translated in the imperative. The invitation to participate with heaven invading earth would read, "Come, Your kingdom; be done, Your will!" Operating in the call of God is an invitation to live with this imperative. **The call is an invitation to partner with heaven to bring heaven's value system to earth. It is an invitation to change the atmosphere around us because we demonstrate and declare the presence of the King and His Kingdom.** We each have a choice. Are we going to live with this eternal perspective that has lasting consequence, or are we going to live with a temporal perspective because it makes us feel a little more secure?

The furniture in the room may feel way more real to us than the presence of heaven, but we can be assured that the presence of the King in the room is the greatest reality on earth. His presence is our strength, and when we welcome His presence everything changes. So, make a choice to live in this new reality. Choose to live full of the Spirit. Choose to step into a strategic partnership with heaven.

Our prayer for each one who reads this book is that what we've shared will cause you to grow really hungry to fulfill the call on your life, hungry to step into all He has destined you for. If you are hungry to fulfill His call, then invite the Holy Spirit right now to invade your life with fresh revelation. Father, we declare that from this moment there will be an activation of Your call in every aspect of our life and a revelation of our destiny as recruits in Your special forces. We release a revelation of our calling as those who spend our life expanding the Kingdom of Heaven.

William Booth, founder of the Salvation Army used to say, "I am not waiting for a move of God; I am a move of God." We understand that when we walk in our calling we make things happen. This confidence comes as we walk in partnership with heaven. Every believer in every profession has this kind of call available simply by responding to the wooing of the Holy Spirit. We begin to take responsibility to be atmosphere-changers instead of waiting for something to happen.

God has extended an invitation to each of us to come into a strategic partnership with Him in extending His kingdom and bringing in the harvest. The time of waiting is over; it is now **time to fulfill our calling and destiny.**

Endnotes

1. Oswald Chambers, *My Utmost for His Highest* (London: Marshall, Morgan & Scott, 1972), 15.

2. Timothy Keller, *Every Good Endeavor: Connecting Your Work to God's Plan for the World* (London: Hodder and Stoughton, 2012), 19.

3. Brother Andrew, http://www.sermonindex.net/modules/my-album/viewcat.php?cid=357&min=120&orderby=titleA&show=15 (accessed 3/18/17)

4. Ian Thomas, *The Saving Life of Christ* (Grand Rapids: Zondervan, 1972), 143.

5. Henry Parry Liddon, *Sermons Preached Before the University of Oxford, 3rd ed.* (London: Rivingtons, 1883), 279.

6. Ravi Zacharias, *The Grand Weaver: How God Shapes Us Through the Events of Our Lives* (Grand Rapids: Zondervan 2009), 65.

7. Os Guinness, *The Call: Finding and Fulfilling the Central Purpose of Your Life* (Nashville: Nelson 1998), 34.

8. John and Sam Eldredge, *Killing Lions: A Guide Through the Trials Young Men Face* (Nashville: Nelson, 2014), 9.

9. Andrew Murray, *Abide in Christ: Thoughts on the Blessed Life of Fellowship with the Son of God* (London: James Nesbit, 1888), 32.

10. Paul Billheimer, *Destined for the Throne, A New Look at the Bride of Christ* (Ft Washington: Christian Literature Crusade, 1975), 16.

11. R G Letourneau: *Mover of Men and Mountains* (Chicago: Moody Press, 1967), 205.

12. John McElroy, *Passing on the Baton* (Cedar Rapids: Arrow, 2006), 20.

13. John C. Maxwell, *The 21 Irrefutable Laws of Leadership Workbook* (Nashville: Nelson, 2007), 226.

14. Amy Carmichael, *Things as They are: Mission Work in Southern India* (New York: Young People's Missionary Movement, 1906), 43.